DOWNLOADS FROM THE AFTERWORLD

by

G.J. BIRMINGHAM

ISBN: 979-8-9901995-0-7
Paperback
First Published: 2025
First Printed: 2025
Published by: G. J. Birmingham

Contact Author: G. J. Birmingham

Email: gjbirminghamneopoet@gmail.com

TikTok: @gerardbirmingham1

YouTube: @g.j.birminghamneo-poet1834

Instagram: @g.j._birmingham_neo_poet

Facebook: @gjbneopoet

DEDICATED TO:

The Most High God of the Universe and the Afterworld, who had inspired and guided me to produce this work.

My father Henry Birmingham (deceased).

My mother Gloria Birmingham.

TABLE OF CONTENTS

EMOTIONS

INSPIRATIONAL

RELATIONSHIPS

PHILOSOPHY/EDUCATION

RELIGION

ODE

NATURE

SOCIETY

WORKPLACE

MEDICINE/HEALTH

PANDEMIC POETRY

SCI-FI

EMOTIONS

TIME THE TREADMILL

I start each new day
With my fuel tanks
Full of confidence and drive
To efficiently fly through
A freeway of chores.
The first on my list,
One task scarcely done.
Time overtakes me
The day's doors all close.
Hours which passed by
Felt like minutes gone.
Dizzy from the rush
Of running around
Trying to keep up
Hopelessly in sync
With the clock's rhythm.
I slip and tumble
With a sore body
And fractured spirit
Into the cold arms
Of stoic fatigue
Reflecting hard on
My unstable mortality.
An end that can come
In a shocking flash
Since time refuses
To bargain with me
In turning down the speed
Or shifting to reverse
So that I can feel
Deeply accomplished
As a fleeting spark
In the infinite

Blazing fire of aeons.
Then I realise
In an anxious woe
With a humble hue,
That time is a treadmill
Moving way too fast
While I get nowhere.

BROKEN FOCUS

My glass full of focus
So fragile by being awkwardly placed
In a precarious position
On my table of endeavours,
Has now fallen onto the floor.
Shattered fragments stare up
Glistening into my panicked eyes

OH! WHAT WILL I DO
TO GET BACK ONE SO PRECIOUS
SO THAT I CAN CONTINUE
TO MAKE UPWARD MOVEMENTS
ON THE LADDER OF SUCCESS?

I look around me
In frustrated dismay
As I see my fervent progress
Wither and disappear
Because I allowed
Galaxies of distractions
To pull my insatiable senses
Towards every cardinal point
And end up distractedly dizzy
Waking up erratic judgement
To knock over the gift of focus
For which I now mourn to return to me.

DISTRACTIONS

I drove down the smooth road
Paved with a supporting mixture
Of determination and goals.
The traction of my car's tyres
A perfect fit with the ground's surface
Carried me in untiring confidence
Towards the destination of my desires.
But as I reached halfway there
An unforeseen unpleasant surprise
Flew out of the bordering bushes
And blindsided me **BAM**
Off my steady cheerful course
Onto a crumbling path
Which awakened the ire of my car
And my dormant anxiety
To knock out my peaceful focussed vibrations.
I struggled to stay strong
To return to my ordained course
Using every drop of my energy
In my reservoir of effort.
I knew that the journey back
Would have been a hard draining one.
But my unshakeable hope whispered
That I will return soon, and arrive
On time at my finishing line.
I just had to look more and more
Into the mirrors of vigilance
To monitor the furtive movements
Of the lurking monsters of distraction
Which awaited the commands from the council of hell

To mercilessly pounce upon me
And pull me away in a flash
From the bright blessings
Standing in patience, several miles in the distance...

THE PROCRASTINATOR

I'll do it in the next second
Maybe I'll wait until the next minute strolls by
Or when sixty of them accumulate
But as twenty-four groups of sixty march on
Through the roads of sunlight rays
And blackened pathways of night
My body still remains stagnant
With bright open zealous eyes
And a mind factory manufacturing ideas
To move forward, upward and soar high.
The stingy body refuses to spend a drop
Of its currency of energy
To manifest what the mind had made
Into the physical realm.
For the body in its arrogant misled belief
Thinks that it rules over the mind.
Vain body has forgotten
That it is an enslaved and addicted junkie
To the words "later" and "tomorrow"
The progress- defeating duo
That keeps the body and mind in conflict.
As every aspect of time repeats itself
With infinite energy on and on and on and on,
My efforts to move in grand passionate strides
To the hills of success and beyond
Still have amounted to nil.

MOTIVATION GONE

MOTIVATION! WHERE DID YOU GO??
You left me without saying anything
I thought that we had a strong bond
As a diligent energetic team
To make a positive mark as lifeguards
In a world drowning in negativity,
In the hope that we can resuscitate
Some kind of soothing balance
To the goodness of the universe.
Your absence has left me distressed
With ceaseless nervous anxiety
That has numbed my creativity
And has left me to sink slowly
In the quicksand of lassitude.
My mind is now filled with a fearful fog
That obscures all beauty inside and outside of me.

MOTIVATION, WHAT DID I DO TO DRIVE YOU AWAY FROM ME??
Was it my pile of extravagant demands
To move forward too quickly
Into the realm of success?
Did you feel that I took you for granted
As I selfishly sucked up your loyal energy
And did not consider your needs at all?

MOTIVATION, WHAT CAN I DO FOR YOU TO RETURN??
I can grovel shamelessly for hours
Hoping that my words of regret
Will thaw your now frozen heart.
Maybe I can make a friendly deal
To lighten your heavy burdens

So that you can work in peace with me
For the benefit of both of us
For years upon years to come.
I could also just sit and wait in faith
That you would come back soon
With open loving and forgiving arms
Ready to embrace new beginnings
So that we can continue on our special mission.

MOTIVATION, PLEASE COME BACK!

DESERTED DREAMS

You were a gift delivered to me
By diligent angels
Who had the unwavering faith
That I could bestow upon you
Showers of nurture and care
So that you can mature
To bear fruits of wonder
For all who hunger
For deep invigoration
Of inspiration to ascend
The steep gradients of life.
Sadly, you arrived at a time
When my life was haphazard.
Crowds of chores and routines
Lassoed me from diverse directions
Pulling me with painful selfish forces
To pander to their insatiable needs,
While I repeatedly neglected
The magic that we could have made.
My heart sank like a jaded stone
In muddy waters of abandonment
When I saw you starving
And crying out for grains
Of my attention and love.
The bright sharp hues of your face
Had become faded patches,
Mere ghosts of their past glory.
Your body's strength eroded
By the friction of my disregard.
I lay all burdens of blame
Upon my numbing shoulders
For the abuse that you endured.
I know that my regrets could never

Restore life into you again.
Nor will my mourning
When I watch with aching eyes
As you disappear into nothingness.
I will surely pay for my sins of omission
From now and into the hereafter
For my gross mistreatment
Of the blessing granted to me
By divine powers now disappointed.

THE STEREO LIFE

My life is a stereo.
I can adjust the volume control
To enhance my situation at the right time.
Vibrations which come forth
Are in sync with moods and drives.

Volume at zero,
I feel the peace of silence
Priming me up to blossom.
In this silent zone,
I await patiently and prepare
For the next phase of my life.

vOLUME INCREASING,
My efforts and rewards
Increase simultaneously.
Synergistic allies,
Unyielding artisans carving out
Success at each rising level!
AT FULL VOLUME!!!!

I have reaped my rewards
But they have become too overwhelming
And have been attracting nemeses.
Thus, I turn the **V O L U M E d o w n**
To reflect on my next move.

CONTOURS

Hardships have laboured long,
Ploughing deep lines into my face.
Scars of tribulations endured
Throughout my long journeys
In trying to let my colours bloom
While facing constant bombardment
From many obtrusive obstructions
Hurled by a pallid world.
One may look upon those lines
In a fit of raging disdain
But they do tell long truthful stories
About my life's turbulent history
Which my tongue cannot compare
To describe in a river of words.
At least respect those tracks as I solemnly do
For they are trophies of a life well-lived.

I'M GLAD THAT WE MET TONIGHT

The wide open doors of this dive bar
Welcomed me inside to partake
Of varied volatile spirits
Imprisoned by walls of glass
Where from my command and bail money
I had set them free and then to become part of me.
As dimmed multicoloured lights stared
Out of spaces within the dark air
And pulses of rhythms and melodies
Broke out of large black boxes,
Your smile shone like the Sun
And beckoned me to come closer
To your angelic presence.
Our minds intertwined in erotic bliss
As we deeply discussed the mysteries
Of nature, time and space
And the complexities of humanity's existence.
Our energies and wavelengths were in sync
As we felt relief from the burdens of banalities
From deserts of cacophonic conversations
Which try to numb our minds
In every routine day.
Flocks of hours flew past
Though they only seemed like a few minutes.
We bartered sweet dreams and phone numbers
As we strolled out of the diligent doors
Which opened and closed
Bidding a quick farewell wave to us.
We will meet again very soon oh angel
For I am glad that we met tonight.

LAMENTATION OF THE LOVING MENTOR

After so many years
I had been your sandpaper
Using my rugged studded nature
To smoothen your rough potential
Exfoliating your negativity,
Transforming it into dust
To be kicked away by air molecules
So that you'll never be hindered again.
I shaped you diligently
Exposing your true beauty
So that you can use your gifts
To inspire downcast souls.
Now that I am worn down
From my hard continuous work
In purest patience and love
Enabling your development,
Why do you now crumple me up
And discard me into oblivion
Without even a droplet of thanks?
Not that I am pleading for it
It's not that I need it at all
What hurts me most is that I feel
An important part of my work
Was in tremendous vain.
My efforts never inspired you
That you weren't stimulated at all
By my humility and grateful nature.
I hope that you'll break free one day
From the chains of pride's trance
And embrace righteousness of heart
To maintain your karma eternally
Overflowing with virtue.

INSPIRATIONAL

SEGUE INTO A NEW DAY

Morning's eyes are opening up
Those of night closing down.
Zone between light and darkness created
For a seamless transfiguration
Into another calendar day.
Living kingdoms start to scurry
Into their divinely scripted roles
In mass vivacious anxiety
To perform an age-old rigid ritual;
Obeisance to an awakening Sun
As it stretches its rays
Beginning its routine rise
Elevating in the east
And embarking upon its journey
Towards the welcoming west
To kindle and inspire
Varied dreams and goals
In every niche of nature,
Thence to rest unseen in its cradle
Obscured by a nocturnal blanket.

CARPE DIEMAGIC!

WAKE UP! The morning is blossoming!

WAKE UP! Caress its glory awakening!

Don't lie there like picture of gloom
Let your faith take you from your horrid tomb.
Life is a cycle, each day ain't the same
One day suffering, next day wealth and fame.
Don't hide from the brilliance of passion
Let it infuse you with inspiration.

Your mind is pregnant with magic ideas
Through royal birth, they will soon appear.
Don't tangle yourself in your net full of fears
Break away now and erase your tears.
Turn away now from those childish nightmares
You have more than anyone else has here.
Shoot your wisdom straight into their ears
Your perfumed words will make their lives clear.

Triumph has won you in his fight
And now grants you a renewed might.
Sleep with victory now, you'll be kept warm
And given zeal to conquer your storm.
Travel high with your gifts of radiance
Quench the masses' thirst for confidence.
They will unite with you in synergy
For a new spiritual liberty.

THIS IS MY DAY

This is my day
Given to me as a gift
I will hold on to it
And would not let it go.
I have earned it in fairness
From the blood shed
During marathon sessions
In long weeks of labour.

A suffocating office
Where hills of papers
And beeping digital devices
Had stolen my energy.
With rising anxiousness
I have waited on this day
To be my peaceful escape
Into the empire of relaxation.

I will pick in abundance
The fruits of affirmations
From the orchards of positivity
To reclaim my lost vigour.
I will dance with soothing winds
Embrace the heavens' warm rays
Absorb the birds' sweet serenades
And stare in peace at wild bouquets.

My broken soul will be healed
The pieces will reunite with love
This is my day
I won't let it go...

THE SEEDLING

Here I am briefly in the comfort
Of a coated womb that feeds
And protects me from the dangers
Of the harsh outside world.
Air, water and warmth
Nurse my minute fragile body
To drive my growth and development
Out of the doors of dormancy
To ascend bravely towards Heaven
Guided by the light of the Sun
And anchored to the rugged soil
By my network of rootlets below.
My tiny branches shall spread out
In deep zealous thanksgiving.
The little green leaves attached
Will all capture raining droplets of light
To help me to claim my independence.
I shall patiently await adulthood
Able to transcribe my individuality
Expressed in many versions of me
In continuous repeating cycles
Here in the long expanse of time.

A PARTY

I wanna' throw a party
No celebration really
Just to fill the empty holes
Scattered on my soul
Created by the erosion
Of my weary emotions
In conflicts with a contrary world.
It would make everything right again,
I believe this with all my shrinking strength!
I want the cake and ice cream to invade my mortality
And replenish my energy
To tread with confident hope
Along the broken roads of life.
The music, balloons and dancing
Will certainly elevate my spirit
And enlighten it with enthusiasm
To connect with my waiting dreams.
I know that my grand party
Will continue to resonate with me
In a long-lasting positive after effect.
All who I invite will be guaranteed
A share in the portion of renewal
And be in harmonious unity with me
To move forward and grow in success and happiness.
If only I had the resources
To make this party a reality
I could move forward, to be a better me.

THE POWER OF ONE

One drop of water
Started a raging flood
But quenched the driest thirst
Of thousands of drought-filled lives.

One racing teardrop
Down the face of a saddened child
Darkened the mood of a whole family
But united all members in caring love.

One spark burnt down a flourishing forest
Its mass murdered all forms of life there
But it brightened up a blackened night
That guided the lost safely to their destinations.

One short whispered word
Out of an innocent mouth
Stirred up a discussion of wisdom
And changed society's way of thinking.

One puff of air out of a tiny nose
Created a squall across the land
It clobbered everything in its path
But subdued the scorching heat.

One leaf fell off branches high
And hit the ground beneath
It hindered the grass' growth by blocking the light
But it's decay fertilised the seedlings of future trees.

THE LEADER

MOVE FORWARD! FOLLOW ME!
I use very few words in my service.
My actions by example do the speaking
They are driven by the trinity
Of humility, integrity and practicality.
My energy radiates from my body
To draw us all together
As a powerful team
To analyse the theme
Of the blueprints of this vision
And be the architects of the goals
To construct a world rich in positivity.
I am not here to condemn, nitpick, nag, dictate
Or fill you with false hopes
And burdens and stress
Which will throw us off our mission
And destroy all of our positive efforts.
I am here to share my gifts
Of experience, guidance and motivation
All enkindled by my love and respect for you.
As you come forth to follow me now
My example will grow in you in time
And blossom into stellar beauty
To become what I am now
Just as I did from being blessed.
By being inspired by others
Who had preceded me in this journey.
Those who also extended the invitation
With an abundance of actions in service
And a pinch of the words
MOVE FOWARD, FOLLOW ME!

THE MOUNTAIN

I grew patiently
In a slow careful rhythm
Climbing towards the pinnacle
Of a resolute maturity
Close to the comforting sky
With thin air and thick clouds
Over a million years
Amidst varied changes
In climes and cycles
All diligent artists
Which have embedded
Their creative toils
With loving tireless hands
Upon my anatomy.

My cloak of species vast
Has called me its home.
There have been times
When part of this garment
Had been ripped away
But restored with new patches.
Then unwelcome scenarios came
And stripped me naked.
My hard scarred body exposed
But without shame and sadness.
For I awaited to be dressed
In a new and glorious garb
To again stand out and shine
In a renewed beauty.

At this present time,
As your feet touch me
With gentle rhythmic beats

Moving upwards against
The grasp of gravity
To reach the top of my head
And get closer to the heavens
In a shorter time than me,
I support you in love and strength
As your journey strips away
Your cumbersome burdens
And you become attired
In the royal fabrics
Of happiness and peace.

I SAT AT THE EDGE OF A CLIFF

I sat at the edge of a cliff
The steep forehead of a cold mountain
Where the panorama and I kissed in profound passion
With our piercing gazes
While a choir of breezes
Exhaled high-pitched sighs of relief
In unison with me
As I gave up in glee
The memories of the discord
Of the flat land that lay miles beneath
Which would never be able
To muster up droplets of energy
And rise up in confidence
To experience the joyous peace and success
That lies way above it.

I shoved little custom-made love notes
Written neatly in cursive love
Into retired empty bottles of sedation
And passed them into the hands of gravity
Which delivered them in haste
To the serpentine rivers below.
I waited in hope that some forlorn souls
Would seize one or maybe more
And absorb the words therein
Which would be the answers
To their SOS's and maydays sent out to the universe.
They would gain the strength and courage
To abandon the surrounding chaos
And ascend that formidable mountain
To keep me company at the edge of the cliff.

SHADES OF GREY

My heart hurts for those
Who only see black and white
Either or and all or nothing
Switching on and off
Back and forth
That's it...
I lament that they have blind spots
For the varied shades of grey;
Perspectives gradually ascending
From the dark and into the light
Which bridge the yawning chasm
Between the two extremes.
As my eyes travel forth
Along the links between the two
Major points of view,
The sundry changes in hues
Make me deeply treasure
Those unsung ignored heroes
Which bring harmonic balance
And unwavering stability
That boldly bolsters up
The reign of the black and the white.

WISdom's Eyes

Last night whilst I scurried
Across the cold floors of my home
Trying to salvage and savour
The rapidly flowing remnants of time
In that cycle of twenty-four,
Wisdom flew out of nowhere.
Its angelic wings flapped
With smooth and silent grace
Into my illumined sanctuary.
On a rugged table it rested
With its broad wings closed
In an upright pride to reveal wide open eyes
Printed deeply on their tender surfaces
With spellbound stares like a contemplative owl
Upon my startled eyes
Which then returned the gesture.
My mind's eye then wandered back
To the hours before night strolled in
In the midst of the all-seeing Sun
When I was drowning in ignorance
But praying and thirsting for knowledge
To carry me forward along
The pathway of enlightenment
And grow together with nature.
An answer to my prayer, a blessing
Had arrived in quiet dark hours
In the form of a humble being
With wings adorned with caring eyes
To inspire and give me hope
In my devoted quest to become wise.

OCEAN OF OBSCURITY

I drove through meandering miles
Of stony roads neglected by human labour
Across rigid hills replete with greenery
And slopes with haughty gradients
To go to a sea that has been shunned
By a population that thrives contented
With close comfort zones of shallowness.
As I arrived and my feet stamped my signatures
Across the lonely galaxy of white sand,
Blackened rippling water beckoned me
To approach and feel its silent power.

My toes touched its fizzing borders
And I felt a welcoming warmth
In deep contrast to the widespread rumours
Of the eerie coldness that sustains it.
My fears tried to clench me
And begged and warned me not to dive in
"For the water's blackened body
Hides varieties of hideous mysteries
Which will destroy your naïve soul."
I scowled and escaped from my fears
And dived into the deep dark waters.

As I looked around, the watery black walls
Supported me with modest care.
My mind was cleared and ready
To receive new knowledge known by only a special few
Who did not fear to venture in bravery
Into these waters which held arcane truths
Too great and complex for unequipped minds.
Oh, how thankful I was for the courage!
To overcome my arrogant apprehensions

And immerse myself in the depths of obscurity
To see lights of truth hidden there.

CLUB SANGUINE

The doors of this exclusive club
Are open wide to welcome
All those with heavy crosses
Carried with pride and hope on their strained backs
Arched by the hands of pain.
These mortals of strength and honour
Despite their drawn-out tribulations
Show passionate glowing smiles
Spread across worn out faces
Which have grown accustomed
To the prolonged friction of grinding gears
Of the machines of abuse.
Their loads of hardships
Are their VIP membership cards
Which they present at the entrance
After they walk across the red carpet
Dyed with the blood of resilience
And the same colour as the premium wines
Which they will drink with gratefulness
To celebrate their strength in coping
With the harshness of life's realities.
They show no remorse for their antitheses
On the outside of ruby velvet ropes
Who yearn in agony to get a tiny taste
Of what awaits the queue of elites.
If only they had given them support
Instead of prodding with bars of negativity
Then they too could have partaken
Though on a much smaller scale
In the all- inclusive feast that lies beyond
The open doors of paradise.

THE ARTERIES OF BLESSINGS

As I eagerly travel through
Long enclosed tunnels
Paved with red undulating carpets
Leading me to my desired blessings
Which I have poured out in prayers,
Obstacles of curses block me
In domineering defiance.
I look at them and laugh
In a mocking display
As I forge with relentless skill,
Bypasses around the stubborn nuisances
And continue in merry victory
Along my path to claim with pride
My grand prizes which await with love.

THE CANDID CANDLE

Speak softly to me
O candle in the dark
With your flame engrossed
In a wavy pole dance
Upon an ebony wick
Within the agitated air.
Stimulate my indifferent heart
Into a motion of love.
Shed your waxy teardrops;
A cocktail of joy and sorrow
Down your statuesque frame
As I feel your illumined grace
Brilliant with truth and serenity
Draped all around my presence
And blocking the disrespect
Of the domineering darkness.
My lens of focus is now cleansed
By your small but powerful light.
Your bold and bright presence
Connects me to the powers on high
Which yearn for my words of praise
And my modest requests
To take my life to greater levels.
But as your moments shorten
I thank you for your sacrifice
By offering a glistening tear
Which reflects the last flickers
Of your dying flame...

THE LIGHTBEARERS

There are rare people here
With brightly glowing auras.
They are oases of light
Who venture out into the human deserts
Filled with darkened souls
Deserted by spirits of love and joy.
On the luminous beings' journeys
Impoverished ones direct their attention
To the lights for which they crave.
Some are drawn to the passionate lights
Like an insect to a beacon of fire
And then steal some of that greatness
To quench their blackened thirst or hunger
But they will still be dim in glory.

There are those who shun the light
Their distorted faces and blocking hands
Show their profound disgust.
For their collections of sins have been revealed
Which they toiled overtime to conceal.
Their rages break out of their prisons
To try to extinguish the light
In fits of deceit or violence
But the deeds backfire to worsen
Their painful dark miseries.
Though drained by those interactions,
Those with the light move on
And will grow even stronger than before
As their hardships fuel their brilliance.

ANGEL IN TRANSIT

An honest man and a loving woman
Had a child who brought them a joy
That they never had before.
A relief from their years of abuse
By the hands of society.
On a thunderous rainy August night
The sneaky hands of death came
And grabbed away their precious one.
The grieving parents cried and wondered why
This misfortune had befallen them.
One quiet sunny Sunday morning
As they lay down on their crewcut front lawn
Hanging out with thriving roses and daisies,
Their eyes connected with a plane
Flying through the southward sky
Quickly away from them.
Memories of their honeymoon
Opened their mouths in soft conversation.
They reminisced of going in transit from New York
To the island of Tobago
A hybrid gem of green emerald and blue sapphire
Where the warm air stimulated
Their passion to conceive.
Their minds then wandered back
To that beautiful child that they loved.
Then an awakening flew into their thoughts
That their departed child was an angel in transit.
Spending a short time on the Earth
To fulfil an essential spiritual purpose
Before going to its final eternal destination
Where it will be in service to God
To maintain and enhance His universal laws.
This revelation squeezed some more tears

Out of their interlocking eyes
But those were tears of joy
From the appreciation of the experience
And thankful about knowing
That they were chosen to play a role
In their sweet angel's promotion.
They looked again to the sky
Smiling at their beloved
And watching their sadness fly away.

RELATIONSHIPS

THE DOWNCAST ANGEL

You try to fly
But your wings are numb.
You try to cry
But your tears are frozen.
In this monarchy of empty souls
You have been chained and gagged
By its despotic ignorance
So, you focus on the demons of the world
Who cunningly lure you
With their jewels of deceit.
You try to find happiness in them
But their distractions
Hide their true evil ways
Which they'll use without mercy
To cripple you into submission
And to detain you deep inside
Of hell's playground.
Oh downcast angel! Give me your jaded hands.
Let me infuse your soul with my wisdom
So that you'll soar
Even higher than before
And blot out all evil
With your sacred light.
Trust in me, for my words are true,
I was a downcast angel once
Just like you...

THE RESCUE

I saw you drowning
In your ocean of anguish
Waving your arms
And screaming for help
Tossed around by the turbulence
Of the turbid waves of pain.
I dived right in and brought you to safety
To the heavenly shore
Blanketed with warm sparkling sands
Of comforting tranquillity
That worked together with me
To scrub away your fears
And resuscitate renewed life
Filled with glowing hope
Into your battered being.
I cannot accept your thanks though
For I must shower you with praise.
I was in the midst of an accident
Almost hit by speeding cars
Of neglect and indifference.
Your distress distracted me
And made me quickly transfigure
From being a wayward bum
Into a fearless lifeguard
And drew me in a spontaneous flash
Towards your battle for survival.
Though I saved you from those powers
Which tried to destroy you,
Your uncertain state
Saved me from my own
And has filled an empty space inside.

THE TRUTH FAIRY

Amidst your pain I brought you fortune
Gracefully in the form of bitter wisdom;
A medicine to counteract the lies
Which have battered your being
And left abscesses in your emotions.
Your stubbornness was hard to extract
It was rooted in a comforting fear
That resisted the change to make you whole.
My injection of soft spoken affirmations
Were anaesthetics to your anxiety
To enable me to work with gentle loving care
To cleanse and fill the filthy cavities
Which have long been the ports of entry
Of infectious germs of deception
Which decayed your cognition and conscience.
My deeds will infuse you with a renewal
Of a rich and powerful crowning glory
So that you'll fully break free
From what had anchored you down
Wearily and hopelessly to this place.
You will now ascend to a higher level;
That place that you deserve forever.

THE LIESTORM

Little puffs of lies
Rose from the ground
And ascended to the skies
Over time from all around.
They attracted each other
And merged in strength
With a plan to smother
All truth at any length.
Millions of wet falsehoods
Were rapidly hurled down
To strike all neighborhoods
With a confusing sound.
The lasting floods created
The norms which man now accepts
Lies flow unabated
Leaving our existence bereft
Of the truth that sustained
Our humanity strong
Never can truth blossom again
Once we embrace the wrong.

MANIPULATED

You claim that you love me
And want me to be yours forever
But I see your pain
As it gushes out
With the force of a flood
Out of the holes of your being.
You just really need me
To plug them up
And nothing more at all.
As your pain is now trapped
In dark caves deep inside,
You can rush now
Into the life of the one
Whom you really desire.
But very soon enough
One feeling gone awry
Will cause the pain
To make an escape
And destroy the unity
Between you and your beloved.
DON'T RETURN TO BEG FOR MY HELP!
For due to your manipulation
My own demons of pain
Have become restless
And are breaking out
To destroy what's left of my life.

THE GAME OF THE GASLIGHTERS

Arsonists of your reality
Are guilty of setting fire
To your concrete perceptions and beliefs
Which were fine-tuned by your senses.
They saturate your presence
With thick smokescreens of doubt
Causing your mind to spiral
In a whirlpool of confusion.
The energies of your self-awareness and respect
Fall quickly into their tar pit trap
Sticky and reeking of the filthy air
Of hate, lies and deceit
As their tentacles of control
Wrap tightly around you
To squeeze you into submission
Into their sordid games.

THE UNDERMINERS

Watch them cackling
In dusty dark corners
Stirring up their heated cauldron
Filled with a bubbling soup
From which they take steady sips
Of blazing hot gossip
Into their malicious mouths
To throw at the bullseye
Exposed on their target's rigour.
A fiendish effort to subdue
In sabotage of blessed work.
They obscure their idle traits
By creating an unholy illusion
Of them being saints of diligence
While making the truly dutiful one
Appear as the lazy villain.

I CAN'T USE YOU... SO I HATE YOU

I badger those around me
Who I think are naive and weak;
Wearing my conquests of them
As badges of honour
On my erratic heart.
I throw my fake smiles
And words coated in sweet frosting,
Feigning love and gratefulness
To get anything that I desire
Whether or not I really need it
Good or bad do not even matter.
It just depends on my momentary mood
And to temporarily subdue
The gluttonous beast inside.

But frustrations stab me all over
When I interact with you
A person so strong in character
My voodoo can't work on you though.
You discern with the sharpness
Of a finely crafted sword
That cuts through the front
Which I had created painstakingly
To hide my true intentions.
Your resolve is a thick and firm wall
That I cannot penetrate or scale
With my tools of cunning or deceit.
Thus my rage becomes a wildfire
Whenever you are close by.

Nausea circulates within me
Like a runaway tornado
When I see or hear your name

Or any letter in its construct.
When I hurl my missiles of aggravation
To damage your confidence,
They dissipate into nothingness
Before they reach your presence.
I will put up barriers of indifference now
To protect my inflated ego
Filled with the hot air of discouragement.
I will now watch you with my arctic eyes
Bleeding with hatred
While feigning my disregard.

THE HATERS

They hate you ‘cause you’re tall
They hate you ‘cause you’re small.
They hate you ‘ cause you’re pretty
They hate you ‘cause you’re ugly.
They hate you ‘cause you’re happy
They hate you ‘cause you’re angry.
They hate you ‘cause you’re confident
They hate you ‘cause you’re diffident.
They hate you ‘ cause you’re taken
They hate you ‘cause you’re alone and broken.
They hate you ‘cause you’re quiet and calm
They hate you ‘cause you’re a loud alarm.
They hate you ‘cause you’re poor
They hate you ‘cause you got so much more.
They hate you ‘cause of your hair
They hate you ‘cause there’s none up there.
They hate you ‘cause you’re brilliant
They hate you ‘cause you’re ignorant.
They hate you ‘cause you’re moving up
They hate you ‘cause you’re about to drop.
They hate you ‘cause you’re overweight
They hate you ‘cause of your skinny trait.
They hate you ‘cause of the God you praise
They hate you ‘cause of your faithless ways.
They hate you ‘cause of your aptitude
They hate you ‘cause of your lassitude.
They hate you ‘cause you’re brave
They hate you ‘cause you live in a coward’s cave.
They hate you ‘cause of your youthful age
They hate you ‘cause you’re an elderly sage.
They hate you ‘ cause you’re strong in physique
They hate you ‘ cause your body is weak.
They hate you ‘ cause you’re well

They hate you ‘ cause you’re sick as hell.
They hate you ‘cause you drive a car
They hate you ‘cause you can walk very far.
They hate you ‘ cause you’re a truth teller
They hate you ‘cause you’re a lie seller.
They hate you ‘cause you’re perfectly clean
They hate you ‘cause your dirtiness can’t be unseen.
They hate you ‘cause of your tattered attire
They hate you ‘cause you’re a walking fashion empire
They hate you ‘cause well...this is true
They hate you ‘cause you’re you.

THE HATER'S VICTIM

HIT ME HARD TO OPEN MY EYES!!!!
To see what's happening behind the lies.
In front of my face, empty affection
Behind my back, total destruction.
I was much too blind for much too long
I didn't notice what was going on.
Bright lights keep on dimming all around me
Can't find any comfort in reality.
Those who call me lover, those who call me friend
Really want to see my happiness end.
SHAKE ME UP NOW I WANT TO GO AWAY!!!!
Don't want to stay here another day.
Cold dark shadows tease my sanity
And torture me with their greed and envy.
Any time I try to keep the peace
I get struck down by the selfish beasts.
Bright lights keep on dimming all around me
Can't find any comfort in reality.
Those who call me lover, those who call me friend
Really want to see my happiness end.
BANG GOES MY EXPLODING RAGE!!!!
In my maximum frustrated stage.
Though I conquered intense pressure and pain
Those around me want my strength to wane.
Slamming into their barriers makes no sense.
Got to crush their evil in my defence
Bright lights keep on dimming all around me
Can't find any comfort in reality.
Those who call me lover, those who call me friend.
Really want to see my happiness end.

LA BASSE

You thought I didn't see ya
Didn't cha?
You thought I didn't notice
Not so?

The glistening jewels
And bright silky garments;
Decorations on a dumpster.
Floral fragrances on your skin can't cover
The stench of your inner negativity.
A landfill site devoid of love
With vermin of hate scurrying around
On piles of decaying slanders
And envious attacks on innocence
Which created your personal history
Of which you are not ashamed
Because you have no conscience.

It exiled itself away from the destruction
In your midst that you cannot see.
'Cause the thick black smoke
Emanating from the fires of your iniquities
Thoroughly blinded you.
You attract vultures who orbit around you
In gleeful patience
For they lack discernment.

Their senses cannot penetrate
Through your flimsy masks.
I am glad that I am distant from you
Away from the eyesore and odour
Of your wicked troubled spirit
That you try to conceal

By tawdry trinkets and aromas
Which fool others but not me

You thought I didn't see ya
Didn't cha?
You thought I didn't notice
Not so?

AN ANGEL IMPRISONED

WHAM!! THERE IT IS AGAIN!
Your hand on my face
Which should be caressing it
With all the affection of your being.
Instead, your infection of rage
Unleashes the wildfire of pain
In every aspect of my existence.
My tears pour profusely out of their wells.
They are strange solutions of love and resentment
Which baptise the new scars born
And defile the old ones resurrected.
OH LORD! ANOTHER DAY IN THIS CYCLE OF TORTURE!!
A revolving door of horror and agony
Through which I tread wearily and fearfully
When I should be as happy as the risen Sun.
Your hateful words pound my soul
Like a vicious thunderstorm.
Your loud, dirty curses and insults
Rain down rapidly and sting and stain me
Creating tattoos of shame on my emotions.
Day and night your gaslighting ignites
The dormant fuel of confusion deep inside
That I question the integrity of my sanity
As I pray to exorcise the demons of abuse
Out of this union with you.
How long can we wear our smiles as masks
And post pretty social media pics
To fool the world about our lives?
The poster children of perfection, right?
The same illusions which you created
And I fell mesmerised helplessly into
Now cause me to lose my mind

As I see behind the scenes
Of your deceptive play
While I continuously receive
Blows upon blows, kicks upon kicks
From your sickening anger.
As I venture out to secretly seek help
From those granted gifts to uphold the law
They slam indifferent doors in my battered face
My pleas for help as I beg
please, p l e a s e, p l e a s e
Can't thaw the cold hearts of the authorities.
Where did I go wrong in my life?
Why did bad karma come to haunt me?
How can I break out of this prison
And spread my wings to fly free again
To go forth to find the beauty that I once had?
I want to go far, **f a a a a r** away from you now
To a safe place where I can peel off these wounds
And start a brand-new life in peace.
But though I try with all that's left of my might
Unseen bonds between us can't seem to break.
I can wait in hope for this bondage to disintegrate
But one more strike...
WHAM!!!!! It may be too late...

IN MEMORIAM...

I cried at your funeral.
My eyes bled with tears
As I stared at your rigid lifeless face
Poking out of your shiny casket.
An avalanche of joyful memories
Cascaded down my mountains of elation
Into the valleys of my conscious mind.
Our delightful times spent together
Were glowing angelic testaments
To heavenly love and friendship.

Days after, while my heart still mourned,
Several leaves from the branches
Of your kith and kin
Blew onto my doorstep.
They told me and showed me proof
Of your devious plans
To grind me into crumbs
Thence to exhale in rage
With a passionate hatred
To scatter my remains into oblivion.

A scrapbook of tattered photos
With us together draped in bright smiles
But with mascaraed X's censoring
My dilated loving eyes.
A black leather-robed diary
Revealed red, fancy fonted words
Engraved in delicate white pages
By the diligent nib of a fountain pen.
My name repeated in uncanny companionship
With words describing my organised demise.

My head now bows down
Not in respect for your remembrance
But in profound agony and humiliation
As I recollect our happy times
And rip them up in my storerooms of reminiscences.
I was so foolhardy and carried away
By the special bonds which we shared.
I ignored the little red flags
Which were warning me in profound vain
About your trap to which I was indifferent.

I want to pull you out of your urn
And disperse you into the blazing wind
That flies along that seashore
Where we reinforced our alliance
In a regular rhythm over the years.
You have now earned my disgust
As I scream out your hideous name
Covered in my slimy spit in vengeance,
To diffuse light years away
Into the infernal crevices of emptiness.

GOODBYE, I AM GONE

Why did you give your all to others
While you abused me with your indifference?
And every word I poured out of my soul
As a gift to connect to you
Was beaten down to a hard death,
But the words of others were embraced lovingly.
You need not be bothered now
You won't hear my voice again.
I know that it annoyed you
You don't have to tell me lies;
The sight of me will be a blur in time.
I know that it annoyed you
You don't have to tell me lies.
I have served my purpose here
Whatever that may have been
Just a lonely life walking through a desert
With no oasis anywhere in sight.
Those focussed dreams which kept me afloat
And ambitions which I had tried to build
To help to improve the state of the world
Had all been destroyed by unseen hands
I guess to make room for your favourites
To get their way with much less effort.
In a nebulous region of the vast universe
Why do you mourn my absence
When my presence wasn't celebrated?
Why do you now eulogise my efforts
When you trivialised them when I was near?

A TENANT SCORNED

HMPH! KEEP YOUR DAMN OLD APARTMENT!
From me you'll never get a cent.
Rooms where you can't spread limbs and dance
Too small even to hold ten ants.
Four whole walls full of massive holes
Through which a striker can score goals!
Those squeaky slack and rotting doors
And creaky, jaded, dirty floors
All sing with gross melodies flat
With every sly mouse, rat and bat.
I'm glad that you don't want me here
I'll take myself and things elsewhere.
A humble home will serve me well
Far from this bland conceited hell.
I laugh now at your scowling face
As I depart to a new place.
My eyes would not be cursed again
BY YOU AND YOUR UNHOLY DEN!

STEAMY SEXY POSE

I saw my love in a steamy sexy pose
On the internet with all exposed.
My baby embarrassed me
Let everything out for all to see.
It was done for money, and done for fame
Done without pride, done without shame.
Now my feelings are hurt, I'm filled with woe
'Cause my honey, honey is now for show.

What will mommy say will daddy frown?
Now my angel, angel has been dragged down.
For my eyes only, now my love will never be
Many greedy eyes will overtake me.
Sweetheart sweetheart goodbye goodbye
A storm of tears for you I will cry.
I lost my love to money and sex
And now my boo is rated X!

Philosophy & Education

IN HONOUR OF THE MASTER CALLED CHANGE

Change...the constant in the formula
Of natural existence.
Both a mysterious magician
And an eminent engineer
Dictating the rollercoaster ride
Of perpetual time.
Creating cycles of chaos and order
In varied seeming contradictions.
As quick as a lightning flash
Or as slow as a snail's journey.
It may sneak up unpredictably
Or show its works gradually.
Its effects may be microscopic
Or take on a gigantic form.
They may be short-lived
Or sometimes show illusory permanence.
All in all, change is immortal
It can transfigure into different forms
But yet still retain its royal name
And function in each unique situation
So that the collective works of this master
Will forever maintain the balance of nature.

ERUDITE...

Each little lesson learnt daily
Is a brick that I lay
To build my castle of wisdom.
I know that this castle will never be complete.
My mortal lifetime is too short
To fully build and furnish such an abode
With the infinite library of knowledge
That is humongous compared to a puny human
With an insatiable hunger
For deep enlightenment.
However, I live in peace and gratitude in knowing
That my castle, though incomplete,
Will be a testament to my accumulated knowledge
Accrued over my lifetime's expeditions.
A crude wonder in the world of erudition
An incomplete Taj Mahal based on love of learning.

WRITER'S BLOCK

A convoy of shining words
Racing rapidly through my mind
Won't be arriving today
At its solemn destination
Where the words would have been used
In the construction of inspiring writings
To deeply stimulate various emotions
In multitudes of readers;
Connecting them with the rollercoaster ride of life.
The convoy has reached a high extensive wall
Placed suddenly and boldly in its path.
The construction site has become a desert
Scattered with skeletal fragments
Of retired words and ideas
Which can never be revived,
But replaced by the demons of clichés.

A team of inspiring images
Tries to demolish the frightening wall
As it bombards it relentlessly
With wrecking ball forces
Trying to let the fresh batch of words through.
But its persistence collapses
And it disappears into an obscure void,
But the wall still stands firm and strong.
How long will this humble writer wait
For that wicked wall to disintegrate
And let the right cargo of words
Come forth in that grand convoy

To its rightful destination?
I wait in passionate hope
That the wall will soon be no more
And my treasured art will be restored.

THE WRITER'S ROAD TRIP

Why don't you drive a car?
Well, my vehicle is my pen.
I steer its slippery nib
For miles across
Blank paper roadways.
On these smooth paths
I can DUI without penalty
Inebriated by my impetus
To release the energies
Of my thoughts and emotions.
Ink is the magic fuel
That sustains my journey.
Accidents are x'ed out
No harm done to anyone.
I drive in straight rigid lines
And I swerve in fancy curves.
Out of this adventurous ride
A work of art is created
With miles of sparkling and varied words
Brought together in coherence to stimulate and inspire.
Indeed, a far cry from
The routine dreary rides
On the nation's burdened roads
Were fumes of exhaustion,
Bitter fear and anger pollute in cooperation
Forming an unholy cocktail
That drunkens all souls present
Until they become numb to all goodness.
Hey, break away for a moment!
From the asphalt rodent race
And use my special car for a new escapade!

RELIGION

THE CORNERSTONE

There was a lonely stone
Laying on cold and jagged turf
As towers of success were being hastily constructed
With materials of flashy glamour.
The stone pleaded with profound might
To play a small but skilful role
On this grand stage of victory.
But the builders ignored its wishes,
Kicked it around and struck it with spit
In cruel and spiteful disdain
For that which wanted just a little chance.
In time, the buildings were beaten
Punched in every part of their bodies
By freeloading elements as they passed by.
The beauty bruised and crumbling
Was stared at by the saddened stone
Who had survived unscathed.
As royalty rolled into town
With its idolising golden entourage
To create new opportunities
For the past glories of success
To return to their reign,
The stone felt warm cushioned hands
Embrace it in deep love and lifted it up high
Above an audience of multitudes
As a strong voice spoke with divine authority
That this stoic stone
Will surely be the cornerstone
Of the new prosperity
For the honest humble-hearted.

Oh! This stone sustained in strength
By nature's harsh but caring pressures
Felt relief with a modest peace
As it was placed in subtle calmness
In its new and eternal abode.
A small comforting castle of space
For this eminent cornerstone
To support in angular jubilation,
A legendary triumphant future.

THE WEEPING MESSIAH

I am the Lord your Master, your God.
Why have you struck me with your wicked rod?
After I created you out of my love and image
You shunned me like a leper and stopped your homage.
You blame me when everything always goes wrong
When it has been you to blame all along.
With your complacent conscience and lack of faith
You always breed calamity and hate.
My people can't you see?
I'm the weeping Messiah shedding tears for thee.

Why have you continued to eat the forbidden fruit?
And deafen yourselves when I speak the holy truth?
You now wave your palms to worship the outcast snake
Every rule and commandment you seem to break.
In my church, the ones I've put in authority
Have let me down with their loss of sincerity.
Money and scandal have hurt my ministry
Have they forgotten their vows of humility?
My people can't you see?
I'm the weeping Messiah shedding tears for thee.

Why was my gospel misunderstood?
Everything was written for your own good.
You cannot change it around to suit your need
To fulfil the need of your evil greed.
Don't you care about my beautiful plan?
Why be obsessed with the laws of man?
After the cross, I still feel the pain
My people I hope you'll follow me again.
My people can't you see?
I'm the weeping Messiah shedding tears for thee.

HEAVEN'S ANGELS NEAR TO THE GATES OF HELL

They all know that the Messiah
After His spirit left his body on the cross
Descended into hell;
A mystery to mankind.
Oh, why would the Son of Man
With a spirit radiating with the purest of light
Go down into the infernal pits
To be sullied by the air of vulgarity there?
Little do the curious minds know
That He came down here
To visit, thank and motivate
Us angels from Heaven;
A special arm of the army of God,
That travails in the vast region
Near to the gates of hell;
The zone of transition
Between the Heavenly paradise
And the cursed nation of the underworld.

We monitor, stalk and capture
With supernatural keenness,
Those errant and damned souls,
Which try to escape in haste
From Satan and his demons' grasps,
To barge their way into Heaven.
We send them back en masse
Via the overworked but willing ferrymen
Who are captains and navigators
Of the veteran skiffs which slowly traverse
Across the flowing magma
That makes up the rivers of hell.

We are hunters of slippery souls
Hurled down from Heaven's gates,
By orders of St. Peter,
Which try to run and hide from their fates,
Cooperating with cunning defectors from hell.
We prowl and hunt them all down
Mercilessly, with every drop of our energy
And ship them out moaning and pleading
In agonies magnified
Across those flaming rivers
To their rightful destination
Where their investments of sins
Over their wicked lifetimes
Will be thrown back at them
With compound interest
In multitudes overflowing
As they fall slowly and dizzy with pain
In the downward spiral of eternity.

We are ushers of adrift wandering souls
Unsure of their destinations.
We lead them on in surety
Down their correct paths
Based on careful scrutiny
Of transcripts of their profiles
Sent to us by courier doves
From the celestial archives.

We have come to your physical realm
At varied points in time
Garbed in cloaks of incognito
Looking fully human as you do.
By our works, we try to help you to focus
On living righteously to seal your connection
With the Most High One abovc.

Those who follow our example
Will ascend past the zenith of the sky
To be forever with their Maker.
Those who mistreat and betray us
And innocent mortals,
Those who ignore and denounce
All of the Heavenly powers
In a lifetime of constant crucifixions
Will be branded with the wrath of the Divine
And be sent way below the universe's nadir
Where they will see us again
And with our arms wide open.
We will grab them and throw them
Onto an awaiting ferry
That will carry them to live
With their evil tribe
In perpetual suffering.

PREPARATIONS FOR THE REIGN OF THE ANTICHRIST

Just as plants need the nurturing elements
Of sunlight, air and water
And a comforting soil to call their home
To thrive and fulfil their role in nature,
So too does the unholy one
Who will come forth from hell
To enslave the souls of mankind
Needs an ambience to sustain
And comfort him when he comes
To maintain success in his reign.

CLIMATE CHANGE comes forth
And raises the heat far and wide
Close to that of hell's atmosphere
To create pleasing work surroundings
And soothe the skin of the dark tyrant.
POLLUTION of the air, water and land
By the indifference of Man
Desecrates and destroys
The purity of nature's beauty and truths,
And creates an ecosystem of death
Akin to the abode of Satan's offspring
Who will come to rule in terror.

The dark spectre called **IGNORANCE**
Flies furiously into the turmoil
To assert its wicked power over Man
With its cargo of doublespeak
And flimsily fabricated narratives
To be fired by the cannons of popular media
Which will annihilate in malicious rage
The grand vaults of knowledge

Constructed by the truthful wisdom
Of legendary great sages
Throughout the vast ages.
God is ridiculed, vilified and banished
From schools and societies
Which then willingly substitute
Empty, tasteless, dry idols
Of stubborn perverted rhetoric
Nullifying any type of moral sense.
A mass of groupthink zombies will be created
By conditioning and the implantation
Of contrary and twisted ideologies
Into shallow insecure minds
To keep humankind in distracted confusion
While it is blind and deaf
To the domineering works
Of the monarch of mayhem
Who will be able to control with ease.

The **SEVEN DEADLY SINS** then return
Riding on horrid horses with hissing fiery eyes
To increase their attributes a thousandfold
By manipulating the created indifference
Of the oblivious members of humanity,
And eliminating all that is holy and just,
Setting the stage for their leader to perform
His wicked deeds across the aeons.

PRIDE is plastered all over worlds
Which are real and virtual.
The lines between them now blurred.
Hubris seething near and far
Giving the clones of Narcissus
Staring into muddy pools,
False senses of superiority

Only to be kicked down in time
Back to a fully real shameful lowliness
By the boots of their oppressor who comes.

GREED pursues every popular luxury
And the money that can buy them all.
It chokes the life out of integrity
To make way for its evil acts.
Adhesive human hands soaked in corruption
Grab and hoard by force or stealth
Until all that has been accumulated
Falls down and crushes them
To be taken by the evil one
To monopolise and upkeep his power.

LUST slithers like a sly snake
In erotic twists and turns.
Its phallic fangs mercilessly inject
Large volumes of the venom
Of warped sexual desires
Into unsuspecting minds
And murders pure and innocent love there.
Fornication, infidelity and rape are celebrated
In pervasive isolated orgies
Which infect the souls and bodies
Of the hedonistic heathens
With germs of indelible disgraces,
But will entertain the evil that comes
As he watches and participates in glee.

ENVY with eyes of green fire
Ignites insidious flames of destruction
Inside weakened hearts and minds.
It is devious and masquerades shamelessly,
Feigning friendship and loyalty

With smiles, flattery and warm embraces;
Cosmetics which hide the evil motives
Of destruction of those with the gifts
Which are sought to be stolen.
Backfired wicked plans
Will make those predators fall and be exposed
Never to be trusted again
And losing all in their immoral gamble.
Their downfall will please their corrupt prince
Who will laugh at them as they become
The dirty jesters at the base of his throne.

GLUTTONY force feeds addictions
To every drug and comely food
Which awaken unrestrained cravings
That cannot be quenched
By the spirits of satiety.
Contentment feels like a curse,
Excesses become laws to live by
Until drunken unfortunate bodies
Become so saturated in pain
From the belligerent battering
By those noxious substances,
That they'll remain obese with misery
And be subdued into ignorance
Or even a slow painful death,
So that their new master's plans
Will be accomplished without objections.

WRATH is blood-red wildfire that spreads
Carrying a barrage of screaming words
Of barbaric hatred and profanity
That is captured by the frustrated
Who out of spitefulness and revenge
Act on perceived threats

To their miserable existence
And unleash their terror upon the innocent
Who can't and have done no wrong.
As the victims nurse their wounds in sadness
They become filled with the anger
That they will throw upon other virtuous beings
Who are reflections of what they once were.
As the wrath escalates around the world
The tone is set for the evil one
To rule in happiness without peace.

SLOTH sedates an already wearied mankind
That has neglected the brightened face of hope.
It makes a mass of mundane sleepers
With emotionless eyes opened wide.
Their path to apathy is a religious experience
Sins of omission their gospel doctrine
Painless pleasure in the bliss of nothingness.
The ruthless ruler can now do as he pleases
With no repercussions at all from the masses
In their comatosed existence.

All of those fiendish spirits
Will work together as an infernal team
To produce the new reality
That will solidify the rule
Of that leader from the underworld
Sent by Satan to hold humans in his clutches
In a once beautiful world that will wither
Like plants without their needs.

The ODE one out...

HIPPIE GODDESS

Patches of patchouli oil
Anoint her rainbow poncho
That she got on her Mexican trip.
They throw their little fragrant fumes
Into an asymmetrical room
Where black light beams resurrect
Her pale fluorescent paintings
Back to a new luminescent life
As they cling onto aging walls
From which retired plaster exfoliates.

She swirls deeply immersed
In globular bobbing lights
Projected by a flaring lamp.
Her angelic arms outstretched
And move in slow wavy grace
To rhythms and melodies
Of Eastern and Western cultural hybrids.
She floats on an ocean of higher consciousness;
Though gravity secures her feet on the earthly floor
Her mind and soul in another universe soars.

NATURE

MISTA SUN

HEY MISTA SUN!!!!
What's a-going on with you?
Are you exploding with anger?
Like a miniature supernova?
The **RA**diating **RA**ys of your auro**RA**
RAise a **RA**pturous swelter
Over the Earth's varied matter
As albedo and absorption
Fight for supreme superiority.
In the midst of your spectrum
I feel your sting on my saddened skin
Forcing incarcerated sweat to escape
Out of my tense but open pores
Soaking my skin and attire
Trying to cool my poor body down
And thence to disappear into oblivion
As I am oblivious to focus on my well-being
Trying to hide from the inferno that you unleashed.
OH RA! OH RA!
Great golden Heavenly oracle!
Please lighten my burdens
Of that burning heat that you dissipate
From **SO LAR**ge a distance
But still feeling as if you are next to me.
I pray that you retract
Your shining stingers
In mercy upon this mortal being
OH MISTA SUN!

THE WATER CYCLE

Liquid water flowing on Earth
Greedily absorbs the Sun's rays
To soak itself with warm energy
And change to its spiritual vapour state
Thence to ascend to the heavens
Where it will reincarnate
Into millions of droplets pure
And sprint back to the ground
Eagerly downwards through the air
When they merge at meeting points
To form multitudes of moving masses.
They will take divergent paths
Along the countless roadways of nature
On and below solid surfaces
Bonding with friends and families
Which had remained behind
Or had returned at an earlier time.
Some enter into the lives
Of God's varied lifeforms
To sustain their unique cycles.
After they have done their sacred work
They bid temporary goodbyes
To all that they had greatly served.
They will then repeat the circular path
While the grateful terrain waits patiently
For its blessing to return.

THE CLEANSING RITUAL OF THE THUNDERSTORM

Grey overseers boldly block out
The Sun's daily soliloquy in the heavens today.
They are ready to cleanse the Earth below
Of the accumulated corrupted filth.
They vigorously lash their wet crystal whips
To flagellate the dirty demons
Out of the living and non-living realms below.
As the thin liquid streams strike their targets,
The percussive symphonies crescendo
Into a loud cocktail of wet noises
Like a thousand machine guns and marching drums
Blazing explosively into the atmosphere.
The deep breaths of nature are exhaled
Creating eerie moans and whistles.
Erect structures erratically wobble
From the liquid and gaseous impacts.
A crooked electric scribble of light flashes
Like an illegible note written by a Heavenly doctor.
Then a **BIG BOOM** from above
Like a reverberated bass drum kick
Comes through celestial loudspeakers at volume max.
Thirty minutes hence, the rhythmic decrescendos
dominate
Thence disappearing into quietude.
The overseers move onwards
So that the Sun can continue his daily performance
And also expose the glossy layer
Of cleanliness over solid nature.
The post-tempest perfume of earthly petrichor
And choirs of birds singing recessional hymns
Herald the ending of the cleansing ritual.

LES CORBEAUX

Watch them elegantly ascend
Towards the sapphire sky
Like hundreds of black boomerangs
Forming a fluid inky vortex
Soaring in circular slow motion
With the courage of gypsies twirling
In a ballet around axial air currents.
All parties in powerful unity
Expressing grace before the meal
In a graceful but excited dance above
Celebrating and confirming their feast
That lays lifeless and sequestered
In the sepulchre of a dense forest.
The time has now arrived
For them to climb down
From the high airs above
To assemble around their repast
And quench the fires of their hungers,
Erasing the sight and scent of death
To make room for the birth of new beings
Which will one day also become a part of
The patiently waiting dark angels.

SEA GAZER

I cast vision's net upon
The infinite horizon
Where sky embraces the sea.
I trawl for the scenery
Highlighted by waters blue
Beauty understood by few.

Waves rise above ocean's floor
And crash on the stagnant shore.
Their final foams cleanse the sand
With hissing kisses unplanned.
The tides encroach then subside
By moon phases they abide.

Boats and ships skate to and fro
On the surface as they go
In diverse random journeys
Pushed by fuels or hard breeze
Till they rest at ports and docks
To relieve burdening stocks.

Seagulls and pelicans fly
Soaring, gliding through the sky
Hurling babels of sharp sounds
They converse while making rounds
Scanning waters for their prey
Competition through the day.

Dolphins' pods in graceful dance
Arching forms as they advance
To far goals of mystery
Strengthening their victory
In every diverse venture

Through the hardships of nature.

Oh how I wish I could stay
Diving deeply everyday
In this pristine tranquil view
Absorbing each varied hue
With my eyes like buoys afloat
On this scene I'll forever dote.

PITCH BLACK

I tread through the thick treacle-like darkness
As it seeps gracefully through
The cracks in the walls of dusk
And imbues the submissive landscape
Dressing it in its resting garments.
The dark sweet coolness massages my body
And emancipates me humbly
From the bondages of stress.
My eyes have been given a break
From the crowds of light rays
Repeatedly fighting for attention
Throughout the long day.
Deep dark mysterious sedative!
Embrace me with all your strength
I would not shun you in fear
Like many others willingly do.
They find it hard to understand
The different beauty that you manifest
Which a popular shining day
Could never dream to bestow.

THE ENCOUNTER WITH COLD WINDS

As I walked westward bound,
Crowds of cold winds bombarded my body
But with rapid icy loving embraces
Which tried to convert my forward motions
To those of an awkward drunkard.
Their high-pitched haunting ghostly whistles
Blew erratic chants into my ears
And put me in a frigid stoic trance.
My body vibrated like an aggressive engine
While populations of hairs on my skin
Moved in choreographed undulations
Like a cluttered corn field during a storm.
As the gales all sprinted away in messy masses
Carrying their tumbling baggage of turbulences,
I moved onwards with weariness removed
Accompanied by the sweet tranquillity
That follows any burst of chaos grand.

QUEEN LUNA AND I

She appeared humbly in a dark sky
Without fanfare or applause.
Her large radiant body caught my eyes;
We stared at each other as time flowed by.
The both of us, Queen Luna and I.

She played a starring role on a starless night
Our reflected lights in deep embrace.
We walked together with a graceful might
On each other's strengths we did rely.
Together in motion, Queen Luna and I.

As she descended after hours passed
My memory of her will keep me at peace.
Until she returns from her voyage vast
I know that between us our love won't die.
The love between Queen Luna and I.

FULL MOON CITY NIGHT

Crowds of constellated cars circulate
Through the branching arteries of the city.
Vehicular eyes spew out billions of light rays
To bombard the rapidly raging darkness.
Overhead, the full moon stares down
At the subordinate land beneath her
That appears like rhinestone-studded velvet
Glistening under an agitated mirrorball.
She casts her luminance far and wide
Over rhythmically pulsating specks and sparks
All fighting frantically for attention
On the stage of nocturnal dissonance.

THE ENLIGHTENING UNIVERSE

The universe is a blackboard
Hanging on a wall of disorder
In the classroom of infinity
Scribbled with shapeshifting energy and matter
And their mysterious antitheses
All arranged in a cryptic order
By an almighty entity
For us to decipher
In granular portions
Through the march of generations
To bring us closer to the knowledge
Of the purpose of our existence.

THE SLUMBER REALM

The sandman is here once again
In his peaceful luxurious carriage.
I have paid my toll in tiredness.
Now I'm off to the atoll of slumber
That corrals a lagoon of sweetest dreams.
The shores splashed with delta waves
All in the ocean of nighttime.
My soul is so light and bright
As I lie down in awe in this magical zone
In contrast to the burdensome dark day gone by.
Pleasant **REM**iniscent memories
Form a warm blanket o'er my anxious spirit
As the stress sizzles away into nothingness.
I am now pacified and rejuvenated...
Eight hours here pass by like eight minutes
But strengthens me to battle through another day.
The sandman transports me back with pride in his heart
To the state of confrontational stark reality
As dawn's gates open once again.

SOCIETY

THE BIRTH AND GROWTH OF WARS

Random micro conflicts start
In varied cultural crevices
At random parts of the world
Borne out of reasons diverse.
Just like separated tiny water droplets
Resting on a sheet of glass
Then awakened by agitations unseen
Merge together to form a giant drop,
So too will the domineering hands
Of heartless politics and economics
Provoke those tiny widespread scuffles
And force them together with heavy pushes
To form a large war waving flags of menace
That also sucks in the neutral and innocent
And all resources to feed its parasitic agenda.
It moves like a runaway turbulent tornado
Causing chaos and destruction to escalate
Decimating alliances and needs
Like a pandemic out of control
Around an overwhelmed globe.

REMEMBRANCE DAY

Today at the trinity of eleven
I reflect in deepest gratitude
For the altruistic fortitude
Of multitudes of honourable heroes
As I absorb the choreographed parades
With their overflowing wells of respect
Expressed through each forward step
And uniform angular salutes
Or siren-like melodies from brass instruments
And the thunderous strikes of military drums
Loud as grenades striking battle ground
Or rhythmic rattling firearms
Combined with sonic booms of cannons
Yet powerful like proud heartbeats
In a state of profound respect
For the service of long-fallen warriors
Whose gifts of sacrifice and love
At the altar of each ritual of war
Had sealed the covenant of freedom
For present and future nations.

In distant lands where scars of war had defaced,
There lie vast plains of greenery
Over which air force planes once flew by
Onwards to occupy the airspace
Of turbulent zones of battle
Now draped with bleeding blankets of poppies
On the beds of scattered tombstones.
Those stand at stoic attention
In unison with majestic cenotaphs
On sacred grounds in the civilised world
Engraved with poetic epitaphs
And the noble muster roll of names

Of the brave servants of humanity
All at attention and waiting in patience
Until the army band of Heaven
Sounds a loud bugle call
To signal the day of judgement
To summon all soldiers forth
To fight the eternal battle
Against evil in the spiritual realm.

HALF MAST

A nation mourns again
After a dreadful day of tragedy.
The spirit of distress
Possesses all honest citizens
And holds them captive
In a zombified state.
They are all now distracted
From the purity of positivity.
Heads are hung down
In sadness and in shame
And contemplative respect.
The flags do the same
As they too hang down at half mast
On their long vertebral poles
Nodding slowly back and forth
With a gentle wind's spiritual support.
Soon after the images and clichéd words
Of that horrendously disastrous day
Are washed away by new distractions,
Heads and flags will fully rise again
With a façade of stability
Just poised and waiting
For the next poisonous misfortune to appear,
Then to hang down in helpless submission again...

THE SECOND AMENDMENT

I am the second amendment
In your fundamental bill of rights
Left in the constitutional covenant
Founded in the profound foundry of freedom
By the eminent founding fathers.
My messianic arms outstretched
As an all-encompassing shield
To protect you and your fellow man
From diabolical invaders and outlaws.
Your responsibility is your homage to me,
But blasphemy is using my name
In irreverent disrespectful vain
To justify the shedding of blood out of veins
Of God's innocent angelic beings
Silenced prematurely without reason.
Every drop of their blood falling upon me
Pains me like the bombardment
Of a thousand raging cannonballs
And taints and weakens the power of the words
Which make up my body and soul.
Why should future generations be left
To inherit an ambiguous version of me?
Despite many misunderstandings
And crowds of protracted tribulations
I am strong and I have survived
The long and ragged, rocky roads of time.
I am sustained by the spirit of hope
That my children will properly praise me
With acts of kindness, consideration and peace
For as long as humanity stands...

THE MERCILESS GAME OF CONTROL

They take a heavy-handed approach
By using underhanded means
To keep your eyes off the dirty games
Which have been perverted from the start.
Oblivious you, constantly falling hard
Into booby traps strategically set
To extract every bit of energy
Out of your weary soul.
Your weakness crushes you relentlessly
So that you will never become attuned
To their evil deceitful vibrations
Programmed to destroy all that is good
And taking the asymmetrical fragments
To mutate them into a monster
Presented as pure, peaceful and just
In front of a world clothed in gleeful awe,
But with its true motives hidden behind it
To strip the masses naked of its adoring innocence
And enslave them to labour in misery
Forever in the painful fields of ignorance and lies.

RED HERRINGS BELOW A MACKEREL SKY

The skies of the early morning
Are wrinkled with splashes
Of ripples of patchy little clouds
Which mother nature puffed out
From the depths of her humid lungs.
They all gaze upon the fragmented episodes of life
On the rugged ground below
That stares upwards from way underneath.
For on that chaotic ground
Patches of human clans and cliques
With different schools of thought
Are caught up unwillingly
In the driftnet battlefield
Cast by their leaders aloof
Who unleash their arsenals
Of red herrings back and forth
Which obliterate the sanctity of truth
And create explosions of distractions
Which become addictive to the masses
As they are mentally numbed
To the pains of daily rigours.
The populace now battered by the lies
Is transfixed in a state of stupor
To remain in repeated ignorance
About the selfish agendas
Created by their devious rulers
Who look down in disdain
On their oblivious subordinates
From their high echelons
Which are closer to the sky
With the ripples of patchy little clouds.

COVER UP!!

Someone tipped of the police
So, they made a raid in my town.
For a while they disturbed the peace
While they tracked the suspects down.
Gunfire rang out all around
The wanted were captured after a while.
But then the scoundrels made bargains
With the cops with all their guile.

Dollar bills passed from hand to hand
They thought that the innocent couldn't see.
They looked so obvious with their plan
As they did it so shamelessly.
Thugs can freely roam the streets once more
Raising terror in every family.
Stink and ugly like a runny sore
The system keeps us in agony.

As the wicked get richer and celebrate
Good citizens are left in the mud.
They watch venality accumulate
And spread like a chaotic flood.
Treading through this hell makes us wonder
Where's the discipline? Where did it hide?
In a land with varied views asunder
We can win with integrity unified.

THE STAKEHOLDERS

WE ARE THE STAKEHOLDERS!
We have the power
To drive the stake
Into the heart of the vampire
Which has been sucking
The life blood out of good hearts
For too long a time.
We are the stakeholders
We hold that rigid stake
Ready to plant it into the ground
Ready to support you oh juggernaut
To support you as we light the fire
To burn you like a witch of yore
To watch your hot ashes
Flee in shameless flight,
Your presence to hurt us nevermore.
You reared a career of corruption
"Well done!" you shouted,
An empty praise to yourself
For the damage you have done.
WE ARE THE STAKEHOLDERS!
Without us you are nothing at all
You were our biggest mistake
Now we will watch you fall.

JUSTICE ON AWOL

I saw Justice walking down the street
At a speed surpassing that of mortals
Camouflaged in a grey rumpled outfit
To match the rough aging asphalt pathways.
I ran up to her and asked:" What's up Big J.?"
Her startled shocked countenance stared at me.
Her mouth let out a secret scared "Shh..."
She said:" Pretend that I'm not here.
I have run away from my job.
The broad spectrum of committed sins
The seven deadly ones and then some
Have been increasing at a rapid rate
And have created rivers of case files
Flowing rapidly and relentlessly
To my overburdened work desk.
There is a backlog of penalties
To be administered to the guilty.
That is why settlement is slow to reach
Many a dire scenario.
I hear every shout of the aching victims:
"Why can't I get closure from this?
When would those who terrorised me
Get exactly what they fully deserve?"
The facts about my work situation
Have been strategically hidden
To protect the innocent sufferers.
My suffocation by lack of resources
Such as my rusty retiring scale
And my blindfold riddled with holes
May sadly not ever be replaced,
And collapsing ordered structure
Due to no fault of my doing
Have all made it hard to operate

On a first come first served basis.
To make sure that some kind of work is done
I just pull any file randomly
And toil in diligent overtime
With no extra benefits to me
Until I ensure that the case is closed.
My heart is heavy and I feel tied down
Since I can't create the order that I crave
So that the road of righteousness is smooth
Instead of its present jagged state.
I want the karmic axioms
To shine radiantly once again.
For all victims to revere without doubt
And anticipate and experience
In the shortest period of time
Without despondency or worry:
"All that goes around, must come around,"
"Whatever one reaps, so shall one sow."
I wish I could wait for that day to come.
I know it will motivate me,
But sadly, I have to move on now.
My fatigue is pushing me further
From that nightmare called a workplace.
Let the world fight on its own now
For its own honour and retribution.
Maybe all can be set right soon
Or will humanity's end speed up?
I don't really know, nor do I care.
Deep down in the trenches of my soul,
I can surely say with beaming pride
That I played my part as best as I could.

SCENE FROM MODERN TROPICAL SEASIDE

Electric standing fans set at full speed
Slowly shake their heads from side to side
As they exhale powerful air in frustration
Attempting to push away
The heat that gatecrashed
Into every empty crevice
Which all form a network of mazes
Among the wet agitated patrons
In a sweltering tiki bar
Where grateful varied liquid spirits
Which had been long trapped
In tall glass prisons
Are released indiscriminately
To put their disciples
Under blissful woozy spells.
Outside, the palm trees wave their frenzied fronds
While standing stationary on scorching sand.
They gyrate against ecstatic breezes
As sweet melodic notes soar high
From a solo tenor steelpan
Singing songs of happiness
Amidst the tense national social atmosphere.
The turbid seawater hugging the coastline
Is brown with wastes from man's work on land
As he prepares a terrestrial womb
For the rapid growth and development
Of broods of ostentatious hotels
To house adventurous souls
Who will come forth in speedy glee
To stamp their footprints on paradise....

THE NOISEMAKERS

BOODOOM! Boo Doom BOOM!

BOOM!!!!

BOODOOM! Boo Doom BOOM!

BOOM!!!!

BOODOOM! Boo Doom BOOM!

BOOM!!!!

BOODOOM! Boo Doom BOOM!

BOOM!!!!

Bullying burly black boxes
Sitting arrogantly on tawdry thrones,
Unleash repetitive explosions of sound.
Discordant rhythms and loud echoes
Ricochet randomly across every object
In every direction, far and wide.
Sonic forces bombard my head,
My peaceful state of mind blown to death.
Decibel overdoses are toxic narcotics
Which cause my eardrums to vibrate in pain.
My heart bangs violently against my chest
Like a frightened feral animal
Trapped in a suffocating cage.
The turmoil of anxiety rises rapidly
In sync with the viciously increasing volumes.
Hours feel like slowly dragging days
As I wander in a disoriented daze
When I feel the noise stampeding through time.

My emotions collapse
When eruptions of unpleasant sound
Disrupt my helpless sanity
As it wearily capitulates
To its domineering foe.
No persistent begging or bargaining
Softens the callous hearts
Of the vile perpetrators.
Demons of wickedness and spite
Have possessed them strongly
Because such is what happens
To naturally empty vessels
Devoid of self-respect, esteem and wisdom.

Indifferent authorities
With their white elephant laws
Shut off their indolent senses
From the victims' cries of hurt and anger
Which are loud in sincerity
Yearning for deserved renewed peace.
We are shot down with words
Which should be thrown at the offenders
"YOU'RE TOO LOUD!! KEEP IT DOWN!!"
All we have to empathise with us now
Are the spirits of frustration and despair
As we face another deafening day and night
In a shell-shocked territory
Where we have no shelter
From noise and its minions
As they vainly reign supreme.
But with a flicker of hope
We patiently and humbly wait
For the **BOODOOM! Boo Doom BOOM!**
BOOM!!!!

BOODOOM! Boo Doom BOOM!
BOOM!!!!
To meet its inevitable doom
And make way for peace
Oh sweet peace, to blossom again...
BOODOOM! Boo Doom BOOM!
BOOM!!!!
HAMMERING INTO MY HEAD!
BOODOOM! Boo Doom BOOM!
BOOM!!!!
TO WAKE THE DEAD!

THE DREARY DRIVERS

They sit all day
Every day
Crouched in car seats
Hands grasping steering wheels
Feet tapping pedals.
An awkward dance
To force the vehicle
In varied directions
Under their control
To take them somewhere or nowhere.

They throw harsh cold blank looks
At pedestrians on pavements
Who walk with upright confidence.
Then they grudgingly recollect
That they lack that courage
To tread without shame and worry
On foot at the borders of blistered roads.
So they need that fuel guzzler
To fill the inherent void
That haunts them everywhere.

THE CITY RUSH

Six feet on the ground.
There are three foreigners
At the crossroads of the city’s heart
Who stare gravely with culture shock
On the surrounding erratic antithesis
To their homeland experience.
They are transfixed on the zombification
Of society's subjects
Soiled with the corruption
Of corporate propaganda.
A dejected corps
Treading in parallel, anti-parallel,
Multi-diagonal randomness;
Forming a mass cortège
Through the interlacing pavements
Courting their pending dire death.
Sidewalk loudspeakers hurl happy songs.
They're nothing but disguised dirges;
Smiley faced notes and chords
Which obfuscate the subliminal discord
That will entangle those with wearied emotions
And form a noose
To hang them from
The gallows of shallowness...

RANDOM STRANGERS

As I walk briskly
Along crumbling roads,
Those casualties of neglect
By effete power hounds,
Away from the unholy mix
Of combative sounds and rat racers
Colliding with brutal force
Creating lakes of pollution,
Random folks pass me by
Varied colours, creeds and classes
Move in the opposite direction
Throughout my round-trip journey.
They seemingly sense my despair
Through my cosmetic forced smiles
Protruding chest and wide eyes.
They throw positivity in my direction
Without saying a single word.
Their faces light up like a thousand bulbs
And radiate supporting slogans
"Great to see ya! You got this! Stay strong!"
"You'll make it! You're a winner!"
The energies I receive from them
Switch off my inner darkness
And enkindle the lanterns of happiness
In every aspect of my being.
I am refilled with strength
Ready to take on any challenges coming!
But, on my return to my abode
Those who are connected so close to me
Fix dark frigid stares and threatening postures
Upon my blissful presence.
They stone me with heavy hurtful phrases
"What are ya so happy about?

You owe your life to us!
Go clean up the house!
To start paying back for everything!
Everything that we did for ya!"
I walk wearily away
Trying to dodge their heavy lies
With my head staring at the smooth polished floor
Cared for more by these despotic dwellers
Than they really ever cared for my needs.

SMALL TALK

A staccato of chatters and twitters
Fly out of flapping mouths
Spreading fast like wild confetti
Swerving into unwelcoming ears
Irritating the facets of intellect
In ambitious methodical minds
Which have been waiting patiently
To release newly developed wisdom
And change the riverine course
Of deep contagious conversations
To levels high above ignorant paradigms.
It is those with the sharpest of senses
Who can keenly dissect and discern
The barrages of empty words
Forming anaemic dialogues
Which hide outdated dilapidated veneers
Devoid of nurturing substance;
Numbly engaged in meaningless babble babble
Trapped in fickle social bubbles
Filled with air of fake transient joy.

THE TREND TRAIN

"CHOO CHOO! HOP ON ABOARD!
IF YOU'RE DEPRESSED OR BORED !!"
"CHOO CHOO! HOP ON ABOARD!
IF YOU'RE DEPRESSED OR BORED !!"
Loud comely confident slogans
Loop in roundabouts of sound
From a new train passing by
Down the straight tracks
Of popular history and economics
Which are just as fickle
As the plastic passengers on the platforms
Waiting eagerly to go on board
And experience a new thrill
That makes them feel like royalty
While connecting with the like-minded.
As the crowds ascend the steps
Of illusory supremacy
Waving their tickets in unison
Celebrating their victory over uniqueness
They look back and laugh at those of us
On the sidelines walking our own paths
Filled with the shining light of happiness.
Our smiles and laughter differing
From the irresolute voyagers.
For ours are borne out of honesty with ourselves
While theirs are constructed
To hide the painful fears
Of being ridiculed by each other.
As the train chugs along
And the travellers are amused
By the plethora of pleasures served,
From the hives of buzzwords
Erotically massaging the many tongues,

To the bedazzling embroidered images
Which are stationed boldly on screens
And branded on bodily paraphernalia
Making love to the masses
Which move their hips to and fro dancing
To a smorgasbord of digital beeps and beats
Making a hip sound to their ears only.
As they become worn out and succumb
To their addictions of fickleness,
They stop the train that they are on
To rush out and embark upon another
Seeking the next novel experience.
While those of us on foot
Have ventured many miles further
Into the paradise of contentment.

THEY RODE ON AN OLD HORSE NAMED CLICHÉ

They rode on an old horse named cliché.
The comforting beast of minds sedated.
That group of folks of the same ilk exploited it;
Those who never suckled at the udders
Filled with the milk of knowledge.
Every overburdened tissue of this horse
Was made of recycled words
Which formed colourful phrases
But became pale from overuse
By countless generations.
The back of this old overworked beast
Was mounted each passing day.
One kick and the horse galloped reluctantly
When any trigger or trend flew by
For the clueless cargo
To justify its meaningless agendas
And to mock and condemn its opposers
In a brutal but comical power play
Indifferent to the erosion of the energy
That upkept the horse's efficiency.
One day that poor horse succumbed
To its forced degeneration
And collapsed on the cold ground
Carrying its pile of mindless folks down with it.
Their bones and will became fractured
They had no plan to move on.
Numb to all events and attached emotions,
No remorse for their dead horse,
That faithfully served for so long
That old horse named cliché.

IN EXILE IN MY OWN LAND

When I travel along intertwined roads
Engraved on my nation's face
And give polite greetings
To people passing by
I don't receive any in return.
Those unrequited interactions
Make me feel uneasy
As the summer in my heart
Quickly turns into winter.
My whole being sinks deeply
Into the trenches of sorrow
When I see all others
Exchanging varied courtesies
With the bonuses of smiles
And jovial vocal tones.
Diverse opportunities hide away
When I approach them
To give me a chance.
My diligent efforts downplayed
As if I did nothing at all.
Am I one unseen?
A ghost journeying among
Continuous streams of human life?
Could it be that I have been placed
In a long drawn-out social exile
Destined to be alone
Among the masses
As dictated by unwritten laws
From the judiciaries
Of gossip, slander, fear and ignorance?
Have I been tried and condemned
With no chance for an appeal
In secret courts unknown to me

Based on my unusual differences
In character, mannerisms and looks?
These are natural to me, I mean no harm
But they're contrary to conformity
To the vague norms, folkways and mores
Practised by a confused society
That is content with being shut inside a box
That keeps thoughts frozen in time.
Despite the emptiness in my banishment
I have indeed survived with courage
And will fulfil all my duties in this life,
For the tribulations I faced within my tribe
Have made me grow more uniquely
In grand wisdom and creativity
Which may very well be discovered
And accepted one day in the future
To demolish the present ways
And build new ones to carry society
Into a renaissance of true humanity.

WORKPLACE

THE CORPORATE COMBAT

Skyscrapers grow aloft and aloof
In the feral capitalist forest.
Their canopies obscure
The limelight of success
Of burgeoning businesses below.
Within the grand organ systems
Encased in those gargantuan towers,
Devotees of the dollar deity
Encamped in their corporate champagne rooms
Assiduously plot smear campaigns
Against their multitude of nemeses;
Ludicrous conspiracies against those
Who worship the same god.
Their monstrous feet crush germinating neophytes
Leaving their dilapidated shells scattered
Boarded, battered and scarred
Sporadically across the metropolis
With signs of shame hanging
“Permanently closed” or “foreclosed”
On broken doorknobs or windowpanes,
Signaling the throbbing pains of broken dreams
Of competing for a chance to live.
The beasts are driven by their lustful instincts
For despotic control over the zombified consumer
corps
Attired in iconic images of pseudo pride.
Alive and vicious is this rapacious economic food web
Raping the morals and progress of social evolution
Crippling the revolution of true love and peace
In the starved souls and hapless hearts of humanity,
By the shamanism of commercial shenanigans.

COPROLITE

Long aeons had passed
With you stuck to that same battered chair
Behind an overburdened table
Surrounded by tools of your trade
And despondent exhausted walls
All of which grew agonisingly in age
But remained unchanged
Just like you in this position.
You unleash prehistoric procedures
Daily with overbearing force
Which are in constant friction
With the powerful progresses
That have driven mankind far forward.
You've handcuffed yourself to your post
Exterminating anything new
That comes around your space.
Your aversion to change for the better
Makes you scream in fear and rage
Like a nocturnal blood-sucking vampire
Feeling stinging sunlight on its skin.
Your well-crafted toxic arrogant stubbornness
Prevents you from developing the zeal
To nurture younger ones
Who can move in smooth peace
In your place when your time in this play
Has reached its extinction.
Your stunted subordinates
Are forced by you to dwell
In disgruntled cubicles
With shabby replicas of your furniture
As they try to manoeuvre through
The viscous sticky mass
Of the mucus of bureaucracy

To accomplish pallid tasks
Which will cause nary a ripple
In the pools of advancement;
But for them to earn a pitiful pittance
Way below what they are worth.
They all hope that the day will arrive
When your place here will be empty
Then to be filled with the spirit of development.
But until then you will remain in your position
As a fossil from a time long gone
Right here to maintain the status quo of stagnancy.

DUTY HOUNDS

Conditioned to work, work, work
Under decrepit conditions
With a paucity of resources.
They pant and salivate with eagerness
At every drudging mission
Thrown to them in disgust
By their lethargic masters
Who sit on cushy leather thrones
In offices adorned with sacrosanct logos
And quota charts which boastfully exhibit
Ascensions up ladders of success.
The underlings labour above and beyond
In copious continuous cycles
Day after day, night after night
Ignoring the confines of passing shifts.
Going the extra miles
Like enduring ten obstacle course marathons
And stretching their arms in sadistic pain
To hang their drooping hats higher and higher
Waiting for instructions to jump
Via cold direct voices or memos
Stippled with vague clichéd mottoes.
They get ready to ask "How high" in confidence
As their masters keep on pushing them
To reach Everest heights.
Oversized smiles and no complaints
Obscure their shrivelling souls
Of which they are unaware.
Their connections to loved ones
Have now become
Blurred faded images in foggy memories.
The only links existing now
Are to the manifold overwork

That they howl and bark in pride for
Giving them no droplet of a chance
For even a meagre bonus reward
Or to grow in personal glory
And mingle with the ivory tower communities.

THE BROWN-NOSERS

SQUIGGLE SQUIGGLE SQUISH SQUISH
SLURP SLURP YUM YUM
SQUIGGLE SQUIGGLE SQUISH SQUISH
SLURP SLURP YUM YUM
The shameless sounds of subordinates
Spewing shallow overused compliments
Far up their boss' broadened bum
That was moulded by protracted lassitude.
They sold their listless backbones
For a few crumbs on a mouldy broken table.
They dig deep into the dark side of work
To try to squeeze out some light
With far more of an effort
Than what their solemn wages
Beg them in vain to do.
A strange race to see
Who will get the best of the crumbs
By discarding self-respect and integrity;
Yearning for their brassy reward
Of laying in their master's buttressing bosom
Playing the role of perfect little pets
To sell out their innocent peers
Who may be a frightening threat
In clear reality or odd perception
To the one who wields a nebulous rank
Made up of grandiose words
Written in frosted cursive glory
On a shining glassy bar towered over
By threatening dusty folios.
The diligent turn away in disgust
And give their all for the greater good.
Progress blossoms as they toil
But they are pushed behind thick curtains

To make way for the bombastic show
Featuring those brown dirty faces
Who have humoured the ones above
To move up one shaky rung
On the ladder of hierarchy
Chanting **SQUIGGLE SQUIGGLE SQUISH
SQUISH SLURP SLURP YUM YUM
SQUIGGLE SQUIGGLE SQUISH SQUISH
SLURP SLURP YUM YUM.**
A flatulent mantra released as they ascend
And push their assiduous competition down.

LAMENT OF THE DILIGENT

I'm sorry for working so hard
Climbing above the horizon of duty
With the burdens of your orders
Weighing down on my wearied body
With only my mild smile as my buttress
I'm sorry for that...

I'm sorry for radiating dedication
Inspiring the surrendered downtrodden
Enkindling in them a renewed energy
Refreshed to serve again to keep this paradigm
At the apex of the mountain of success
I am sorry for that...

I am sorry for the fact that as young as I am
I battled distress like a seasoned veteran
The strain that it had impacted upon me
Transfigured me into a stronger version of myself
No longer constrained by your exploitation
I am sorry for that...

I am sorry for the friction between our conflicting natures
Your stagnation and my true dynamism
Leading to a gradual wearing down
Of any remnants of our connection and cooperation
As you blame me for all the shortcomings here
I am sorry for that...

I am sorry for my history of efficiencies
Standing tall in salience surrounding you.
But your senses tuned out my contributions
Perhaps to obscure your fears and insecurities

And to protect your ego from being agitated
I am sorry for that...

I am sorry that soon I'll alleviate your agony
As I leave to ascend towards my higher calling.
Don't let the delay of regret get the better of you
Wallow freely in your flatlined situation
But don't expect my company there
I am sorry for that...

I am sorry that when everything goes awry
And you search far and wide for a saviour with solutions
You'll remember that you drove my hard work and I away
With the greatest of pleasure that you poorly tried to hide
Your barrage of begging will never bring me back
I am indeed sorry for that...

THE BURNOUT

THE UNTAMED FIRES OF STRESS
ARE CONSUMING MY STRENGTH!
Hot gases shoot out of my nostrils
Escaping with rapid anxiety
Hissing like a pit of savage snakes
Angered in provocation.
Muscles are on autopilot
As they vibrate vigorously.
Weary eyes squeeze out teardrops
Which race down my face
All competing to neutralise
The pervasive tensions
Which hold my joys hostage.
The heart rumbles in my chest
Throbbing with frantic frustration
Against its rigid and stoic cage.
My skull endures pulsating pain
Feeling like a thousand jackhammers
Pounding into its inner surfaces.
A random traffic of thoughts
Zoom above the speed limit
On the highways of my mind
Creating convoluted chaos
As they fatally knock down
The pedestrians of focus.
Speeding through multiple time zones
Of a myriad of disordered chores
Ordered upon me by merciless powers,
Leave me in a jet-lagged state
As I zone out and lag behind in progress.
I fail to maintain my mental balance
In my bubble of disorientation.
Year after year, extra miles forced

For every minuscule task
Have compounded a millionfold
But my perks and salary have stagnated.
All systems are weary and weighed down
As if being pulled strenuously
By forces a thousand times
Much greater than gravity.
My body seriously surrenders
To the defeat of the enemy of stress.
Poor body! Laying like a transient corpse
Retired on a comfortable pyre
Waiting until my foe is subjected
To the same torture that I now feel.
OH!!! THE CRASH AND BURN!! THE CRASH AND BURN!!
THE ONLY REWARDS WHICH I HAVE EARNED...

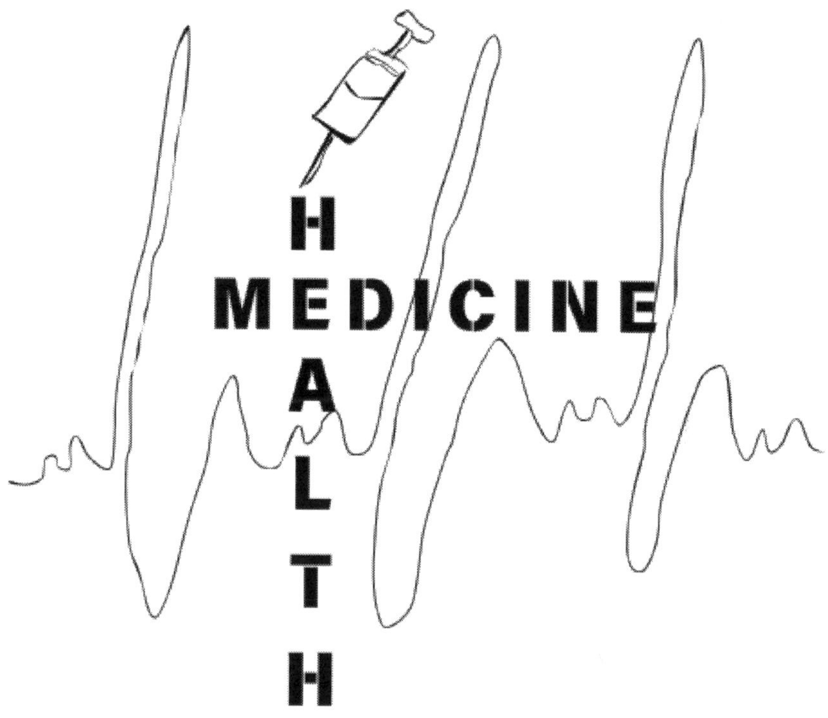
MEDICINE
HEALTH

CONTRASTED LIVES

My limbs are so strong and limber
Filled with infinite stamina.
I walk or run for many miles
In confident rhythms and styles
On flat plains and over high hills
Energy lost, each stride refills.
My mind is knife sharp, can't fool me
It's clear with every memory.
Healthy habits have paid their due
Blessings on me they did imbue.
So great to be well and alive!
At the age of seventy-five.

My bones are brittle, seized and sore
They feel as if they've been through war.
Muscles ache with a throbbing pain
Robbing me of motion again.
I lay listless on my soft bed
Wondering what stress lies ahead.
Dry drooping eyes from lack of sleep
Added on to my troubles deep.
My sighs are signs of self-defeat
I moan with every weak heartbeat.
Oh how long will I suffer more?
It's so sad, I'm just twenty-four.

A NATURAL VIRTUAL REALITY SPECTACLE

THERE HAS BEEN A WAR!!
A VICIOUS WAR WITHIN ME!!
The sweet sugar soldiers
Joining forces with the army of aging
Have wreaked havoc upon my retinae!
My immaculate maculae there destroyed!
The bridges between photonic images
And my mind are no more...
Yet still, what do I see?
Odd lucid hallucinations;
A surreal psychedelic carnival
From some alien realm
Dancing in front of me?
They arouse the demons of fear in my fragile being.
Rigid shapes in bizarre geometry and symmetry
Adrift on a sea of swirling colours,
Appear over the landscape
And form fences between reality and myself.
Unusual people unknown stroll by gingerly;
Silent in manner, small in stature,
All dressed in history's myriad of pompous fashions;
They form a costume party parade.
Their arctic and distorted gazes pierce my soul!
I hail them out anxiously!
But they hearken not my voice.
I try to touch them
And to inhale their scent,
But it is all in vain.
I grab on to my friends nearby,
And shriek "Do you see them? Do you see them?"
But they do not see what I do.

Am I going mad?
Or is my mind trying to cope
With my amputated eyesight?
A phantom vision of fantasy constructed
By strong alliances within my mind
To prevent me from mourning my loss.
After several weird and confusing weeks
I now consider these images as friends.
Angelic allies which defend me
From seeing the real grotesque human wars
In this crazy world.
My fears of this new destiny are now being shattered!
I now embrace this phase of my life,
In my personal virtual reality spectacle
Of this strange but enchanting paradise...

DEMENTIA

A dreadful bane crawled into his brain
With its insidious agendas.
It overthrew the majesty of memories
And sprawled on its throne without shame.
This domineering despot
With its wretched commands,
Unleashed dark destructive forces
In sadistic pleasure
Forming a wasteland of amnesia
By erasing diligent populations of nerves;
The dedicated creators and guardians
Of the golden treasures of the mind
Accumulated over a vibrant lifespan.
It forcefully opened up cabinets
Filled with foul dictatorial laws
To suppress the birth and growth
Of new memories to cherish,
While crushing the circuit boards
Which controlled the entire vessel
To let it fall in gradual weakness and death,
As this twisted tyrant also perished
Smiling with perverse contentment.

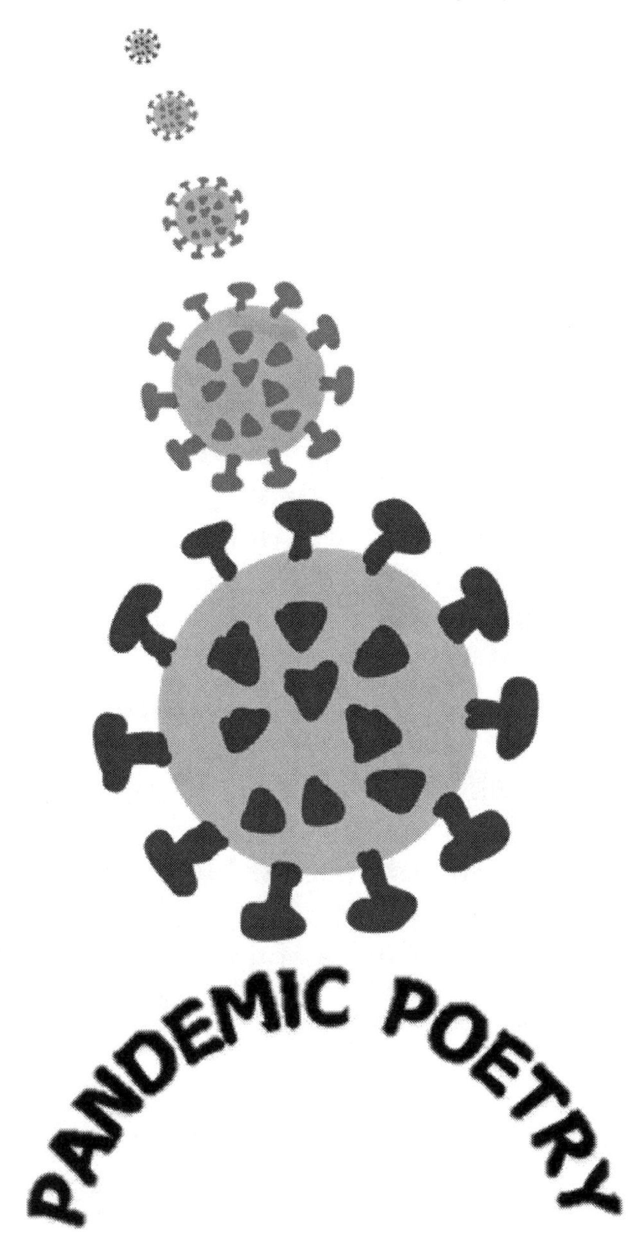
PANDEMIC POETRY

THE GLOBAL INFECTION

PARASITIC NANOARMY!!!!
Strengthened by mutations,
To produce COVID demons,
Leaped high out of an arcane animal,
To wage war upon human nations.
Populations worldwide now becoming invalid,
By the insidious army of COVID-19.
Millions upon millions of nanosoldiers,
Looking like a fleet of threatening naval mines,
Ready to annihilate mankind.
Travelling rapidly by droplet aircraft,
They reach populations of unfortunate cells,
At vulnerable regions of the human body.
They anchor onto ace receptors of their target cells,
With their crown of spikes of terror!
Activated by a temper,
They invade the cells' internal territories;
Tension created in a merciless terrorist attack.
Precious resources are greedily depleted,
To increase the army's relentless forces,
By millions of COVID divisions,
In a selfish virulent vicious cycle.
The immunity army overpowered,
By the wretched villains!
Vile virions engage in collapsing
The system creating the breath of life,
Now a source of unbearable pain,
Before death comes to close the eyes of the victim,
The abused host destroyed...
Amplified army grows stronger every day,
To decimate both the young and old,
And bring sadness to a wearied world.
A large Goliath world trying to retaliate,

Against a microscopic military of COVID Davids,
As each human being, each being a cell,
In the population of the human race worldwide,
Watches painfully as socioeconomic systems go awry.
Each person asking in fear,
"Will this war last for months or years?"
And each wondering when will the nanoarmy strike home,
To desecrate one's life with an unholy syndrome.

FLATTEN THE CURVE

The strengthened viral army comes forth!!
Attacking nations with full force.
Victims flood hallowed halls of health,
To clog up every spot large and small.
Stress amplifies within an overwhelmed system,
Gradually bursting its caring walls,
As the cries of agony and fear
Ooze out through the burgeoning cracks.
The reigning chaos therein
Repels future casualties to their origins
With empty bags of hope for recovery.
Together we must stand up and fight
With strategic solidarity
Against the demonic COVID army!!
To reduce the overbearing burden
Of a system under gargantuan pressure...
Together we must obey the orders
Of the healthcare generals
By going into battle to flatten the curve... to flatten the curve...

Limbo low below the capacity line
Embrace and live the new normal!
Wash your hands and all that they touch
Soap and sanitisers, chemical warfare weapons.
Unleash them relentlessly upon the army of COVIDS!
Kill the COVIDS! Yes, that's part of our mission
Defensive and offensive in our vision.
Flatten the curve.... flatten the curve.... flatten the curve.... flatten the curve....

Go the distance, social distance
From anyone and anywhere.

If you think to socialise now is a chore?
What if the COVIDS conquer you
And you can't socialise anymore?
Stand proud and contribute to the COVID defeat
By interacting with others at six feet.
Flatten the curve... flatten the curve... flatten the curve.... flatten the curve....

Hands off your mouth, nose and eyes!
Don't help the army to enter your insides.
It's never too late to self-isolate
When you feel the heat of fever
Thunderous coughs, wheezes and sneezes.
Hermetically seal yourself like a hermit
In your quarantine cave
So that the army can't advance further
To claim more casualties of its war.
Flatten the curve.... flatten the curve.... flatten the curve.... flatten the curve....

It isn't an arduous task
To wear a protective mask
Over your mouth and nose.
Wear it with pride in your heart!
This divine battle gear
A fortress and a shield in one
A symbol of safety and hope
A powerful blockade to the viral troops
To stop their spread and devastation.
Flatten the curve... flatten the curve.... flatten the curve.... flatten the curve...

Beat them beat them with brutal force!!
And the healthcare curve will be hammered flat
The roads through its system will be smoothly paved.

Wave goodbye to present and future waves.
Let the world create a tsunami of recovery
And blossom into a new age of health and happiness...

THE MASKERADE

The viral army advances,
Trying to migrate,
From air to our bodies,
Through open ports of entry
On our precious faces,
To increase the cases,
Of viral war casualties.
But we've been blessed,
With the best of armor,
Defensive shields in this war!

MASK IT UP! MASK IT UP! MASK IT UP!
From under chin to nose top.
MASK IT UP! MASK IT UP! MASK IT UP!
Wear it well and with pride.
MASK IT UP! MASK IT UP! MASK IT UP!
To keep the COVIDS outside!

Spare a considerate thought,
And wear one made of cloth,
Or the surgical ones;
Both can block out the viral demons.
Masks of strong interwoven threads,
At the frontline facing the dread,
Of the progressing viral army,
And halting its evil journey.
Our simple potent strategy,
Foil the viral plans of tragedy!

MASK IT UP! MASK IT UP! MASK IT UP!
From under chin to nose top.
MASK IT UP! MASK IT UP! MASK IT UP!
Wear it well and with pride.

MASK IT UP! MASK IT UP! MASK IT UP!
To keep the COVIDS outside!

Join together now in this maskerade,
Rainbows of colours and shapes on parade,
All forming a collective blockade,
Against the COVID-19 air raid.
MASKS! Frontal fortresses, facial gloves,
They show our caring love,
For the human existence,
As we use them in united defence,
To stop the COVIDS in their tracks,
And move onwards to take our world back!

MASK IT UP! MASK IT UP! MASK IT UP!
From under chin to nose top
MASK IT UP! MASK IT UP! MASK IT UP!
Wear it well and with pride
MASK IT UP! MASK IT UP! MASK IT UP!
To keep the COVIDS outside!

THE VIRUS WHISPERER

Millions killed in a worldwide war!
Daily death tolls splattered
On the faces of all media
Reflecting the horrific agony
Of the human race besieged
By a morphing COVID army
Moving in relentless stealth
Through innocent vessels
Which diligently try their best
To retaliate in defence
But with a dwindling hope.
If only the distressed masses
Could have an opportune peep
Into the underground scenes
Of laborious science
Where throngs of heroes study
The forms and strategies
Of the invisible killer army
In the course of speeding time.
The blueprints of the soldiers
In their varied states
Delved into and analysed
In the greatest of depths.
Weak spots and strengths
Scrutinised by expert minds.
Data extracted and processed
To build helpful models
And plan a raging counterattack
Using the army's arsenal
Without mercy against it.
The fruits of the labour and plans
Thoroughly tested and mass produced
Fired through arms in grieving humanity

Set stages of preparation
In the bodies of all involved
To conquer COVID troops
As they attempt to invade
With sinister confident zeal,
But to meet unforeseen blocks
And multitudes of upgraded weaponry.
They face a ruthless retribution
In a brutal defeat.

THE AFTERMATH

Relentless insolent pandemic!
Clashes of calamity,
Of man versus virus
Have now subsided
Like tides receding
Into their marine habitats.
The viral army surrenders
In a reluctant defeat
Subdued at the feet of man's ingenuity.
Nanoscopic soldiers now in minuscule numbers
Though trying to devise new plans and weapons
To re-ignite mass destruction,
Have become much weaker than those gone by.
Joyful populations of people!
Now free from the yoke of infections
That overburdened them
In all aspects of their existences.
They now gleefully graduate
From the college of suffering
Into a bright new hope
For renewed health and safety.
They hurl overworked stifling masks
And pungent slippery sanitisers
Into the welcoming air
In triumphant freedom.
Imposed social barriers erased
As humanity returns to express love
In embraces, kisses, shaken hands
Without fear of unseen terrorists.
Amidst the festive celebrations
We must not let our guards
Slip and fall by reckless moves.
'Cause somewhere in dormant corners,

The remnants of the COVID clan
Irked and lurking tenaciously
May be plotting new sinister strategies
To disturb the order once again...
With a rising infectious pestilence...

I CAN'T BREATHE! (2020…STEALING MY BREATH AWAY)

I CAN'T BREATHE!!!!
A new tiny virus came along,
To invade my body and hold me down.
A virus that does not discriminate,
My existence it wants to obliterate.
Wreaking havoc on that part of me,
That creates the breath of life continuously.
I plead for mercy! But it never wanes…
It steals my right to breathe, and fills me with pain.
My struggle ends, no more breath,
As I sadly and quietly yield to death.

I CAN'T BREATHE!!!!
As a big, old, evil virus returns to invade my space,
Holds me down, as my dignity it tries to erase.
This is a virus that discriminates,
My existence it wants to annihilate.
The sadist hatefully presses and forces every breath out of me,
As I cry in pain and desperately beg for sweet mercy.
With my final plea, the anger of the beast violently seethes,
A one-man lynch mob crushes my right to breathe…
Technological vector captures the evil act,
Transmits it virally, and the world reacts.
Humanity becomes shocked, sickened and aware,
Its collective breath halted, in a state of despair.

I CAN'T BREATHE!!!!
I wheeze and cough as though I have some viral disease,
As bulbous clouds of smoke rise above cities,
Out of the fuelled fires of grief and frustration,
Across an anguished and indignant nation.
The world wants to breathe normally again,
The breaths of life, love and peace for societies to mend.
Live in hope! Humanity must stand as one,
To conquer ALL oppressive viruses until they are gone.
A new dawn, humanity will be relieved,
Singing in positive unity! **I CAN BREATHE!**

TEACHING ONLINE IN A PANDEMIC

LOG IN!!
Another day walking on the online tightrope,
Doing a skilful balancing act,
With little training, practise and resources,
To keep curriculum courses vibrant,
Trying not to fall, be hurt or ridiculed,
To the dire detriment of my charges,
With their devices charged and ready for class.
Oh gosh pandemic! You wicked curse!
Shoving me in panic from face to face,
To synchronous and asynchronous interactions,
In the mysterious binary world.

Daily I'm at loggerheads,
With fickle e-devices,
Which do not always cooperate,
On every day in the cycle,
Of the school timetable.
But once my screen illuminates,
The camera captures my image,
The mic configures and transfigures my voice,
From natural to digital form,
It's **LIGHTS, CAMERA, ACTION** mode,
In my mental hard drive's settings.
Put on a brave face and smile brightly,
Hide all fears, angst and pain behind blurred backgrounds,
The online educational show has begun!

My heart roars like an orchestra of engines,
At an auto race in hyperdrive.

Virtual meeting classes are a mosaic,
Of stoic pixelated shots of students.
Periods feel like slow séances,
"Are you with me? Can you hear me?
Please respond. Is anyone there?"
Phrases sound like catchy refrains,
Of overplayed heavy rotation pop hits,
As time within every phase of a period,
Marches rapidly into oblivion.
Multiple tabs open in cyberspace and my mind,
As I frantically try to control,
The smooth flow of my lesson,
Mostly planned, partly impromptu,
Until Murphy's law is prompted,
By trolling digital poltergeists,
To come along and jackhammer the scene,
And smash up my plans to smithereens.

Students in and out, in and out,
Through the revolving doors of routers,
Rendering communication erratic.
Graveyards of deadlines are sparsely filled
With the assignments of students.
Webs of complex issues experienced by them,
Lead to frustrations and conflicts running wild,
Through the jungles of technology.
Pressures mount exponentially,
As they pour down chains of command,
To squeeze out every drop of effort.
I move like a gamer in a cat and mouse online game,
And then account for anomalies in reports,
To be transported via any available medium.

My sight is shocked at an overflowing inbox,
Of e-mails with a myriad of instructions.
Meetings, feedback, deadlines,
Students, parents, principals, school board,
Make me want to declare a state of emergency,
At my overpopulated e-mail address.
Information overload in my drive,
Haphazard scattered files drive me insane.
They are victims of organisational neglect,
Due to my attentions directed elsewhere.
Working hours overlap into personal ones,
Trying to keep up with floods of work,
Which wash away sweet quality time,
For chores, self-care and loved ones,
All in the name of sacrifice,
At the altar of education.

At the end of a day's toil,
Whatever time it may be,
And I log off and try to sleep like a log,
To try to recharge for another round,
My back cries in immense pain,
From prolonged poor posture.
Eyes sore and heavy with vision blurred,
And a cocktail of ambivalent tears,
Cascade down my tense cheeks,
In a live stream of conflicting passions.
Fingers ache from dancing across keyboards,
And working like an octopus' tentacles,
To manipulate multiple devices.
My mind in a state of vertigo,
As the workday's positives and negatives,
Zoom around in circles at light speed.

Day after day, cycle after cycle,
The term finally closes its grand portals.
It's accumulated wildfires of work,
Have crashed and burnt out my body to a char,
And produced a mental blackout.
I've been everything to everybody,
But nothing to myself,
My existence feeling dismissed.
Don't pity me, don't be sad,
I'll tell you what is true,
Amidst the chaos, conflicts and pain,
I did it all, for love of you.
LOG OUT....

SCI-FI

A NIGHT SURPRISE

As my eyes peacefully admire
The beauty of the darkened night sky
Freckled with thousands of blinking stars
And a proud contented full moon
On the never-ending plains
Of infinite light years
I ponder on the many mysteries
Which lay patiently up there
Peeping out of cosmic crannies
Yearning to be discovered.
In my meditative state
A large illuminated aircraft
With a rhythmic pulsating glow
In sync with a loud humming sound
That pierces with an eerie force
Into the heart of night's tranquillity
Appears out of nothingness.
Thence its babes likewise come forth
Which follow their mother in obedience
Towards the west of the heavens.
They flaunt holographic images
Of the beings which inhabit them.
My fear anchors me down
So that I could witness
This special extraterrestrial vision
And receive a gift of initiation
Into the fold of valiant travellers
From a distant and advanced world.

SEA MONSTER

Over long tallies of millennia
A simple small lifeless rock
Caressed by swaying salty waters
While it lay in its sandy bed
Grew and evolved bit by bit
Into a towering beast
With the strength of a million whales
And a crown of brown seaweed.
It now emerges, with thundering stomps
Onto the dry airy land.

Its domineering image
And loud baritone roars of rage
Strike the cowering eyes and ears
Of witnesses beaten by rods of terror.
It has abandoned without regret
The seas polluted by wanton wastes
Bit by bit by indifferent land-dwellers
Now facing their remorseful downfall
As retribution advances in the form of a monster
That they didn't know that they had created.

FURY OF THE NIGHT

Your eyes open to see a hemisphere
Attired in ebony underwear
Looking around ready to seduce
Anything that wants to drink its juice.
It will give you a taste of vertigo
And drag your conscience into limbo
Be alert! Stare deeply all around
Feel the things which will bring you down.

When the dead walk down your street
A graveyard scent surrounds your home.
It gives a profound hypnotic treat
To your mind so that you'll roam
Through misty rivers and frostbite fields
To twist your wisdom and your soul.
To the power of darkness you must yield!
Before your nights start to roll.

The lights from the hills form a compound eye
As it watches you like a hungry fly.
Ready to prey upon your sensuality
To murder its dormant sterility.
The icy winds sting you like angry bees
As you hear the moans of epileptic trees.
YOU WANT TO RUN BUT YOU'RE STUCK IN YOUR PLACE!
Come on, feel the luxury, don't let it waste...

Made in the USA
Columbia, SC
22 June 2025